Conten

G000124421

Introduction

Many people are aware that refined sugars are bad for the health, contributing to dental caries, obesity and other more serious illnesses. Although we are often advised to cut down on sweets, cakes and sugary foods it can be exceedingly difficult. After all it is nice to be able to hand round a tin of biscuits with the coffee, to eat a homemade pudding after dinner and to celebrate Christmas and birthdays with a special cake.

I hope that this book will make the task of cutting down on sugar easier and more enjoyable. It contains over 100 recipes for biscuits, cakes, tea breads, puddings and desserts, all of which are sugar–free. Instead I have used naturally sweet ingredients such as dried and fresh fruits, fruit juices, carob, coconut and spices. A little honey, molasses and malt extract have been included where appropriate, for example in a honeyed sultana cake, an old fashioned parkin and a malt loaf.

The book also traces the history of sugar, describes its effect upon our diet and health and includes a guide to alternative sweetening agents. There is also a section on baking which contains useful tips and practical advice.

Most of the recipes have been created especially for the book and use natural, wholesome ingredients. As a result the biscuits, cakes, puddings and desserts not only look attractive and taste delicious but are also truly nutritious.

The History of Sugar

Refined sugars are the universal sweetening agents, used by cooks and food manufacturers alike. They are widely assumed to be essential foodstuffs and it is difficult to envisage a modern diet without them. They are added to almost every conceivable type of food for reasons of cost, availability, versatility and, of course, sweetness. However, refined sugars have been in general use only since the middle of the nineteenth century.

Before that time man had to satisfy his desire for sweet tasting foods in other ways. Historical records describe primitive processes for making thick, sweet syrups from dates, raisins, grapes and carob pods. It is also evident that very early in his development man learnt the technique of smoking bees from their nests, thereby ensuring a regular supply of honey.

The demand for honey was met until the end of the Middle Ages largely by supplies from monasteries, as the need for beeswax candles made it necessary for the monks to become beekeepers. However, in Britain the change in political climate during the Reformation resulted in a wholesale purge on religious orders and the production of honey fell dramatically. The gap in the market was neatly filled by sugar cane, which was imported from plantations in the New World.

No one is really certain of the origins of sugar cane but it is believed to have been grown somewhere in the Pacific. Its cultivation apparently spread northwest towards Asia and in 325 BC a Greek expedition, in the service of Alexander the Great, discovered a reed 'which makes honey without bees' growing in Persia. The young, tender, sweet tasting shoots were simply chewed and eaten on their own. The older stems were bruised to extract the juice, which was then dried to form coarse crystals similar to those of modern refined sugar. The Greeks clearly liked the Persian reed for they began to import it in vast quantities. Herodotus called it 'manufactured honey' and wrote that it was eaten widely among the rich as a delicacy, as a spice to disguise the taste of old, rotten food and as a medicant.

The area of cultivation increased steadily and by AD 800 sugar cane could be seen growing along the coast of North Africa, on Rhodes and Sicily and in Morocco and southern Spain. It was from the sugar plantations of the Canary Islands and Madeira that Columbus took the plant on his second voyage to the New World. In the years that followed, Spanish Conquistadores and Portuguese Donatórios introduced sugar cane to the whole of Central and South America, where it soon became a valuable crop.

It was particularly important to the islands now known as the West Indies, but overwork and disease took their toll and the indigenous population was decimated not long after its introduction. The sugar plantations were too profitable for the owners to resign themselves to this situation and they looked for new sources of cheap labour to replace the native workers. They turned to Africa and established the infamous slave trade which was to flourish until the middle of the nineteenth century. The historian Noel Deer has said,

> 'it will be no exaggeration to put the toll of the slave trade at 20 million Africans, of which two thirds are to be charged against sugar'.

Although sugar cane could not be grown in the colder regions of Northern Europe the inhabitants were able to sample its delights. The first reported cargo was sent to England in 1319 by a Crusader in Venice at a cost (in today's currency) of £3000 per ton. It proved very popular and was immediately in great demand. However, its high cost meant it was only found in wealthy households and even then was kept in special locked boxes so that the servants (or the master perhaps!) could not use it without the permission of the mistress of the house.

The demand for sugar in the rich countries of Europe was such that when the Dutch and English began to test their naval prowess in the Western Atlantic they became involved in the sugar trade. The Dutch transported the raw sugar cane to newly established refineries at Antwerp and other Dutch ports while the British drove the Spanish from the West Indies and by the middle of the seventeenth century had gained control over the 'sugar islands'.

As a result the supply of sugar to Europe increased dramatically and was followed by significant reductions in price. For example, in 1600 the cost of one pound of sugar was equivalent to a year's salary for a working man, by 1662 it cost the same as three dozen eggs and in 1682 the equivalent to one and a half dozen eggs. This meant it was no longer a food of the rich and could be found in more modest households. Its cost, however, still ensured that it was used with restraint.

Throughout the eighteenth century British and French fleets fought for possession of the 'sugar islands' in order to protect the supplies of raw sugar cane needed for their refineries in Europe. The British brought the matter to a head during the Napoleonic wars when they blockaded the French ports and effectively stopped its importation. Fortunately for the French, reports reached Napoleon of 'a kind of Italian parsnip' reputed to be sweet tasting. He ordered his scientists to carry out further experiments and was duly rewarded when, in 1812, a method of extracting sugar from the bulbous root was perfected. The principal advantage of the 'Italian parsnip', since renamed sugar beet, was that it could be successfully grown in the temperate latitudes of Europe, thus avoiding the problems associated with importing sugar cane by sea. Many acres of French farmland were given over to its cultivation and in subsequent years other countries followed suit. The production of refined sugars increased unabated.

World production of refined sugars:

1839 — 800,000 tons
1900 — 8 million tons
1978 — 80 million tons
FAO prediction 1985 — 100 million tons

Probably the greatest influence upon the level of sugar consumption came from the growth of tea and coffee houses in Europe and America. Such was the popularity of these new beverages that by the nineteenth century they were to be found in almost every home, drunk more often than not with a spoonful or two of sugar. Thus, in a few hundred years, sugar had changed from being a luxury item to an everyday food, regarded by many as an essential part of their daily diet. This trend is clearly reflected in the following table which, although referring specifically to Britain is indicative of a similar rise in sugar consumption in all western industrialized nations. The average Briton or American, however, eats more than anyone else and the figure given for 1978 is representative of both countries' sugar eating habit.

Average consumption of refined sugar:

1588 —   1 lb per person a year
1688 —   4 lbs
1720 —   8 lbs
1780 —   13 lbs
1815 —   15 lbs
1900 —   80 lbs
1965 — 120 lbs
1978 — 120 lbs

Early man was quick to discover that sweetness could enhance the flavour and taste of foods, making them more palatable. Traditionally honey, fruit and syrups were used for this purpose, but they were never produced on a large scale and consequently were used in small amounts. From the vast quantities of refined sugar apparently needed to make our modern diet palatable, one might conclude that the quality of food has deteriorated to a huge extent over the last 200 years. While there may be an element of truth in this, sugar is added not for obvious reasons of lack of quality, freshness or variety but to satisfy an apparently insatiable desire for sweet tasting foods. We have been able to pander to this desire because refined sugar is versatile (being soluble and virtually tasteless) and is cheap to produce. Our consumption has increased to such an extent that some doctors believe that the majority of people living in rich, industrialized nations are actually addicted to this apparently innocuous substance.

SUGAR — FRIEND OR FOE

The range of food on sale in shops, restaurants and 'take away' bars is huge. Exotic fruits are flown in from far-away places; improved agricultural practices have extended the growing season of many vegetables; new types of animals have been bred to produce leaner meat and sophisticated methods of preservation mean that many foods can be eaten all the year round at little, if any, extra cost.

Although cost and availability are still important they are no longer the principal considerations in the selection of food. For the majority of people, in the western world at least, the main criteria are taste and convenience. The experience of eating is a pleasurable one and food is expected to be delicious. Little, if any, thought is given to the nutritional value, for it is widely assumed that food which tastes good must also be nutritious, and that those who manufacture tempting foods 'know what is good for one'. Sadly this is not always the case and increasingly, scientific evidence is showing that the high incidence of many so–called degenerative diseases such as coronary heart disease, diabetes, hypertension, ulcers, high blood pressure, constipation, haemorrhoids, diverticulitis, obesity and dental caries is related to the change that has taken place in our eating habits over the last century.

Greater affluence and the ability to choose the food we eat on the basis of flavour (and convenience) has resulted in an increase in the amount of protein, fat, sugar and processed foods eaten and a corresponding decrease in the amount of starchy carbohydrates.

Anthropological studies have shown that, as societies become industrialized and wealthier, not only is there a fall in the total amount of carbohydrates consumed but also a change away from carbohydrates in the form of starch to carbohydrates in the form of sugar. The following figures for the USA illustrate the point perfectly: in 1889 the consumption of starchy carbohydrates (found mainly in cereals) was recorded as being 358 lbs per head while sugar consumption was 53 lbs per head. By 1961 the picture had changed with cereal consumption falling to 146 lbs and sugar consumption rising to 115 lbs.

The fact that sugar is relatively cheap and increases the palatability of food has not escaped the attention of food processors who add it to such unlikely foods as peanut butter, sausages, fish fingers and tins of red kidney beans. It is used to 'extend' more expensive foods and is said to increase sales. The inclusion of sugar in many so–called savoury foods has played a considerable part in pushing up the level of sugar intake. Although evidence is now emerging to show that sugar consumption has stabilised in both the USA and Britain the average person still eats between 4–5 ounces a day, half of which are eaten directly and the remainder in processed foods.

Another factor that has encouraged the change in our eating patterns is the popular idea that starchy carbohydrates can cause obesity. As a result many people have significantly reduced their starch intake. However, it is only the highly refined, low fibre carbohydrates which, due to their lack of bulk, result in overconsumption and possible weight gain. Unrefined, high fibre carbohydrates such as wholewheat flour, wholewheat pasta, brown rice and potatoes can (and should) be eaten as part of a balanced diet without causing obesity. To appreciate the full implications of our present eating patterns it is necessary to understand certain basic facts about the foods we eat, in particular the role and function of carbohydrates in the diet.

Carbohydrate — the nutrient

There are five basic nutrients found in food, all of which are needed by the body to provide energy and to maintain good health. Carbohydrate is the principal fuel used to meet the body's energy requirements. The other nutrients are as follows:

Fats are an important source of energy but are fairly insoluble substances which cannot be readily absorbed into the body's tissues. Their main function is as an energy store.

Proteins can also provide the body with energy but their principal role is to build and repair body tissues.

Vitamins carry out many diverse tasks, one of the most important being to assist in the absorption of food and its full utilization for energy, growth, repair of tissues and fighting diseases.

Minerals are key components in the structure of vitamins, hormones and cells and regulate essential body processes.

The body's greatest need is for energy, not only to facilitate day to day activities but also to maintain such functions as heart beat and brain activity. The bulk of food consumed is used to satisfy these demands. Carbohydrates are the most efficient source of energy and traditional, unsophisticated diets are based upon a staple carbohydrate food (always a starch based carbohydrate), notably rice in Asia, millet in Africa, maize in South America, wheat in parts of Europe and North America and potatoes in Ireland.

Sugar does not feature in this list of staple foods yet we are all aware through advertising campaigns, that sugar is an important 'energy food' and that the body's blood sugar level is related to the supply of energy. If this statement is taken at face value then the change that has taken place in our diet over the past 200 years must be welcomed, for an increase in the amount of sugar consumed must signify that everyone has more energy with which to 'work, rest and play'. Unfortunately this is not the case and many doctors, nutritionists and dieticians are far from happy about the switch from starchy carbohydrates to their sugary counterparts.

The cause of this misunderstanding is the word 'sugar', which has two distinct meanings. To the majority of people it refers to refined sugar, the white or brown varieties that are spooned into tea and coffee, added to cake mixtures and sprinkled over fresh fruit. To the chemist or nutritionist, however, sugars are a family of related substances, known collectively as carbohydrates. They include simple sugars such as glucose and the more complex sugars (known as starch) to be found in cereals and vegetables. Refined sugar is just one member of this family and is identified by its chemical name, sucrose. The different types and sources of sugars are given in the table below:

The Principal Carbohydrates and their Sources

chemical name	sources
1. monosaccharides or simple sugars	
glucose	vegetables, corn syrup
fructose	honey, fruit, vegetables
galactose	the product of milk sugar (lactose) after digestion
2. disaccharides or double sugars	
sucrose (glucose + fructose)	sugar cane, sugar beet (processed to make refined sugars)
lactose (galactose + glucose)	dairy foods
maltose (glucose + glucose)	sprouting grains
3. polysaccharides or a chain of simple sugars	
starch	grains, beans, vegetables
glycogen	liver, shellfish
cellulose	plants
pectin	ripe fruit

Before the body can convert any carbohydrate food into energy it must be digested and broken down into a monosaccharide or simple sugar. The majority of food eaten in a balanced diet is broken down into glucose and this simple sugar is readily absorbed by the body to become blood glucose (blood sugar) which in turn satisfies our immediate energy needs. The best source of glucose is starchy carbohydrates because they are made up of chains of glucose sugars which can readily be broken down and absorbed into the blood system.

The body has a complex system for maintaining the level of glucose carried by the blood, any excess being converted to fat and stored in the body's tissues until it is needed. These regulatory mechanisms can only operate effectively if the system is not overloaded or disrupted. Unfortunately, the change from unrefined to refined carbohydrates and, in particular, the switch from starches to sugars, adversely affects this control and the natural balance becomes disrupted. The body responds by exhibiting an array of physiological and psychological disorders, known to the medical profession as degenerative or twentieth century diseases.

The problems associated with refined sugars (sucrose) arise not because the body is unable to break them down but because they are consumed in a concentrated form and in unnaturally large amounts. As a result it is relatively easy to overload the system, for by their very nature refined foods, especially sugars, contain little bulk. It is possible to eat large amounts before the stomach registers that it is full and this inevitably results in weight problems. Perhaps this example will help to illustrate just how easy it is to overeat refined foods: in order to eat the equivalent amount of sucrose found in one teaspoon of refined sugar you would have to chew your way along three feet of raw sugar cane!

In addition to the risk of obesity and its associated health problems the consumption of refined sugars can have other effects upon the body. Sucrose is easily broken down into the simple sugars glucose and fructose, and is rapidly absorbed in the digestive system. After eating a food containing refined sugar, large quantities of glucose flood into the system causing the blood sugar level to rise dramatically, far above the normal levels. The body responds to this crisis by releasing large amounts of insulin from the pancreas in an attempt to restore the blood sugar to an acceptable level. Often the pancreas overreacts to the situation and too much glucose is removed, necessitating further adjustments to bring the level back to normal. An individual can experience definite swings in mood and energy as a result of these fluctuations. For example, high concentrations of glucose in the blood can produce surges of energy and high spirits but these quickly change and feelings of listlessness, hunger and lassitude take their place as the level drops.

Drinking sweetened tea or coffee and eating biscuits and chocolate throughout the day simply exaggerates these fluctuations in mood and energy. The strain imposed upon the body's regulatory mechanisms, particularly the pancreas, as a result of this roller coaster effect has been cited as a possible factor in the high incidence of adult–onset diabetes experienced in most industrialized nations.

Many people believe refined sugar to be an important nutrient, essential for energy, but Professor J. Yudkin, an eminent nutritionist has said,

'If only a small fraction of what is already known about the effects of (refined) sugar were to be revealed in relation to any other material used as an additive, that material would be promptly banned'.

In fact our bodies have no physiological need for refined sugar, for it contains no nutrients of any value. However, average sugar consumption represents between 18–30 per cent of the daily calorific intake in Western diets. It is highly probable that as a result refined sugars crowd out more nutritious food from the diet. Andy Warhol once said,

'I'll buy a huge piece of meat, cook it up for dinner and then right before it is done I'll break down and have what I wanted in the first place — bread and jam. All I ever really want is sugar'.

As this rather extreme example illustrates, it is by no means uncommon for sweet foods to be used as a substitute for a balanced meal, thereby reducing the variety and quantity of 'real' nutrients absorbed by the body. This increases the possibility of marginal deficiencies, particularly of the elusive vitamins and minerals. The risk is made even greater because, in order for the body to utilise the energy created by refined sugars, certain vitamins (notably the B group) and calcium have to be available at the same time. Unless these nutrients are available in the foods eaten with the refined sugar they must be drawn from the body's slender reserves. In fact, so thoroughly is refined sugar stripped of nutrients during processing that it scarcely deserves to be called a food. A US select committee in 1973 went so far as to describe it as an anti–nutrient.

Many readers must be wondering whether there are any alternatives to this sweet tasting, but potentially harmful, substance. In fact it really is not difficult to sweeten foods and carry out all types of home baking without it. The secret is to use unrefined foods that are naturally sweet. There are many delicious recipes, from all parts of the world, for sweetmeats, pastries and pies. Many of them date from long before the popular use of refined sugar.

An A–Z of Sweeteners

Refined sugars have gained the dubious distinction of being considered the sweetening agent par excellence. Their appearance, texture, taste and versatility have played an important part in their popularity for they can be used to flavour and enhance almost every conceivable food.

The growth in the consumption of refined sugars has been quite staggering, giving credence to claims that the majority of people living in affluent countries are sugar addicts. However, many people are sufficiently concerned about the much publicised health hazards that they are beginning to look for alternatives. Some switch to brown sugars in the belief that they are less harmful, while others prefer to use honey, reputed to be the panacea for all ills. There is no shortage of information and advice but it often hinders rather than helps in making a decision. The following descriptions of sweetening agents are intended to help the reader through the minefield of contradictory claims.

REFINED SUGARS

It is essential to dispel the idea that brown sugars are superior to white varieties. All refined sugars, be they white or brown, are processed from sugar cane or sugar beet. The refining process is the same in both cases. First, the plant is crushed to a pulp and the juice extracted. The liquid then undergoes a long process of evaporation and crystallization. White varieties consist almost entirely of the sugar known as sucrose, the level being between 99.9 per cent and 100 per cent. Brown sugars contain from 93 per cent to 97 per cent sucrose, the remainder being made up of water, fibre and minute quantities of vitamins and minerals. The distinction between the two is slight and brown sugars do not deserve to be called 'natural', 'full of goodness' or 'healthier'.

White Sugar

White sugar is the end product of the sugar refining process and was originally more expensive than the more crudely refined brown sugars. Early attempts produced a rather grubby, grey looking substance which had to be sold in blue paper cones to give the illusion that it was sparkling white. It was nonetheless very popular with the upper classes. Gradually technological advances led to an improvement in purity and an increase in production. Demand increased when the price fell, following the repeal of the British Sugar Tax in 1874. By the turn of the century white sugar had lost its 'snob' value and was used in most households. Today white sugar can be bought in a variety of grades, including 'all purpose' granulated sugar, preserving sugar, castor sugar, sugar cubes and fine icing sugar. All are equally sweet although those that dissolve the fastest give the illusion of being sweeter. Similarly they all seem to be sweeter when hot and this is the reason why recipes for hot puddings contain smaller amounts of sugar than those for ice creams and sorbets.

Brown Sugar
It has become increasingly necessary to distinguish between 'raw cane' and other varieties of brown sugar. In fact many described as 'light brown' or 'soft brown' are impostors, being nothing more than white sugar crystals tossed in syrup or molasses. The explanation for this sad state of affairs is simple: genuine brown sugar (raw cane) can only be produced from sugar cane, yet 40 per cent of the world's production of refined sugars comes from sugar beet. Raw cane sugars are easily identified because they are dark in colour and have a strong, distinctive flavour. The commonest kinds are:

Molasses sugar — also known as black Barbados, demerara molasses or dark brown sugar. This soft, sticky sugar is very dark in colour and has a distinctive 'rummy' flavour. It contains the B vitamins, calcium and potassium.

Muscovado sugar — called Barbados sugar and 'moist sugar' in America. It is a fine grained, mid–brown sugar containing the B vitamins, calcium and potassium. The most popular and versatile of all the brown sugars, it gives cakes a dark, rich colour and a fruity flavour.

Demerara sugar — is so called because it was first imported from Demerara County in Guyana. It is a light, golden coloured sugar that has large crystals and a mild flavour. A variety sold as London Demerara is made from white crystals coloured with golden syrup and in some cases artificial colouring agents. They lack the true flavour of the genuine product.

SYRUPS

Molasses

Molasses is a by–product of the sugar refining process. Although it can be extracted from both sugar beet and sugar cane, beet molasses has an unpleasant taste and is used principally as an animal foodstuff and in the manufacture of monosodium glutamate. Cane molasses is a dark, sticky syrup containing traces of iron, zinc, copper, calcium, potassium, chromium and the B vitamins. It has a high sugar content but is much less sweet tasting than refined sugars and contains only two thirds of the calories. The strong, distinctive flavour limits its culinary use but it is an important ingredient in gingerbreads and the savoury dish Boston baked beans. The variety of molasses known as 'Blackstrap' should be used with discretion as it has a very strong flavour and is less sweet tasting than other types.

Malt Extract

Malt extract is made from grains which are germinated and then roasted. It is a dark, sweet tasting syrup, traditionally added to porridges and puddings for children and invalids. It is reputed to restore health and stamina and contains proteins, iron, the B vitamins and malt sugar (maltose). A popular way of using malt extract in the kitchen is to bake a rich, fruity malt loaf.

Carob

The carob tree is believed to have originated in Syria but it now grows throughout the Mediterranean. A member of the Leguminae family, it is also known as the locust bean and is said to have sustained St John the Baptist in the wilderness. For this reason it is called Johannesbrot or St John's bread in parts of Europe. It has been valued for thousands of years as a source of food and even the bitter, inedible seeds have been put to good use — they were used as coins in the Middle East and are said to be the origin of the word 'carat', still used by goldsmiths to the present day. However, it is the seed pods that are of the most interest from a culinary point of view, containing sugars (fructose and glucose), starch, fat, calcium, phosphorus and iron. They can be processed to produce a sweet tasting syrup or flour that seems to combine the flavours of chocolate and cinnamon. Carob is widely used in the health food industry as a chocolate substitute for it contains little fat and no caffeine or tyranine, both of which are thought to cause migraine attacks. However it is hardly any better for our general health when it is simply substituted for chocolate in sugared drinks, confectionery items, desserts and oversweetened baked dishes.

Honey

Honey is probably the oldest of all the sweeteners; it was so highly prized by early civilizations that bees and honey were believed to be sacred. They were also used symbolically to represent love and fertility. The Ancient Indian God of Love, Karma, is frequently depicted carrying a bow whose string is made of a chain of bees. In a more practical vein, bees were once credited with the ability to foretell the weather; that is if one is to believe this old English rhyme,

'If the bees stay at home,
rain will soon come,
if they fly away,
fine will be the day'.

Some of the mystique and awe surrounding bees has been dispelled with the development of commercial bee farms, yet honey is still thought by many people to be a wonder food. It contains 181 different substances but, alas, none can be credited with being the elixir of life. Honey consists of approximately 75 per cent sugar (fructose and glucose), the remainder being water and small amounts of protein, vitamins A, B and C, potassium, iron and chromium.

The quality of commercial honey can vary enormously, as can the price. Generally speaking one gets what one pays for but even the costliest jar is good value taking into account the effort that has gone into its production. In order to make a single 1 lb jar of honey the bees have to visit more than 2 million flowers, travelling a total flight path equivalent in distance to three orbits around the Earth and using 3 ounces of honey as fuel. It is generally agreed that the finest honeys are those collected from a specific type of flower, for example Californian orange blossom honey, lavender honey from Provence and heather honey from Scotland. They have lovely, delicate flavours which are unfortunately easily lost during cooking. It is wise therefore to savour these expensive honeys on their own or in desserts that require no cooking. For everyday purposes use a blended honey which has a more robust flavour and is cheaper to produce.

DRIED FRUITS

Drying is an excellent way of preserving foods which otherwise travel badly, do not keep well and have a brief but prolific harvest. They have become one of the principal ingredients in all types of baking, providing additional interest, texture, flavour and sweetness to cakes, biscuits and breads. Their use in sweet dishes is, however, a relatively recent development, linked to the growth in the sugar industry generally.

'Datyes, figges and great raysins' have been used in all the great European kitchens since the thirteenth century when they were imported from the Levant. At that time unusual sweet–savoury combinations were popular, giving rise to such delicacies as ham cooked with apricots, turkey with prunes, veal with dates and the traditional Great Pyes consisting of a mixture of beef, chicken, marrow, eggs, dates, prunes and raisins, all highly spiced and covered with pastry. The traditional British plum pudding or Christmas pudding is founded on this sweet–savoury theme for until the eighteenth century one of the principal ingredients was a large piece of beef.

Apricots

Apricots have been grown in China for over 4000 years but are now cultivated extensively in the Middle East, Australia and California. Traditionally apricots were prepared by splitting the fruit and leaving them in the sun to dry. Unfortunately the fruit became tough and leathery and needed a good deal of soaking before it was palatable. Modern controlled methods of drying, however, have produced a sweeter, more pliant fruit that is soft enough to eat raw. Apricots are full of flavour but are not oversweet, making them one of the most popular and versatile of the dried fruits. They contain protein and fibre and are especially rich in vitamin A and iron.

Currants

The currant comes from a small, purple, seedless grape native to Corinth in Greece. This grape dries easily in the sun and has a hard, crunchy texture. Watch out for poor quality currants containing stalks and sand which will spoil your baking.

Dates

The date is one of the oldest fruits to be cultivated; it is known to have been grown in the fertile land between the Tigris and Euphrates more than 6000 years ago. The finest dates, often referred to as 'candy that grows on trees' are left on the palm tree to sweeten and mature in the sun. They are harvested and packed in boxes with a real (or, more often nowadays, imitation) stalk arranged amongst them. These dates are expensive and are best served as a dessert fruit or *petit four*. Cheaper, loose or boxed cooking dates are perfectly satisfactory for general baking purposes. Dates are the sweetest of all the dried fruits, containing 55–60 per cent natural fruit sugars as well as fibre, calcium, iron, potassium and phosphorous.

Figs

Figs are grown extensively throughout the world and are so common in the Mediterranean that in some parts it used to be customary to allow the traveller to help himself to a fig as he passed by. The dull, rather unpleasant appearance of dried, compressed figs sometimes discourages people from tasting their lovely flavour. The best quality figs are the larger varieties (known as 5, 6 or 7 crown figs) which retain some of the plumpness and succulence of the fresh fruit. Old figs become 'sugary' and tough but they are much cheaper and are useful in all types of cooking. Some packets contain a bay leaf, which is said to keep the figs fresh andd free from pests. Figs have a gentle laxative property and are high in natural fruit sugars and iron.

Prunes

Prunes come from specific varieties of plums, the finest being grown in the Santa Clara Valley in California. They are graded by size, the largest being sold as 20–30s, medium ones 40–50s and the very smallest 80–90s. The figures refer to the number of prunes in one kilogram weight. I prefer to use the larger ones because they become plump and fleshy when reconstituted and naturally contain fewer stones per packet. Until the nineteenth century prunes were far more popular than fresh plums and were eaten with savoury foods such as goose, game and pork. More recently, however, in Britain they have become associated with the unpopular school dessert, prunes and custard, and are generally disregarded by modern cooks. To really appreciate their value one has to take a trip to the USA where they are used to make delicious whips, souffles, moulds, pies and ice creams. They have a natural, gentle laxative effect and are rich in vitamin A, iron and calcium.

Raisins

There are many different types of raisins, the largest and sweetest coming from the muscat grape and known as muscatels. They are expensive and are generally eaten whole as a dessert fruit, especially at Christmas time. Smaller raisins, black, red and golden brown in colour, sold loose or in packets are much cheaper and are suitable for everyday use. My favourite is the Black Afghan raisin. It is seedless, dark in colour and full of flavour.

Sultanas

These are produced from a type of seedless white grape and were originally grown in the region of biblical Smyrna in Turkey. They are softer and sweeter than either raisins or currants and are used extensively in all types of cooking.

ARTIFICIAL SWEETENING AGENTS

Cyclamate

In the 1960s sodium and calcium cyclamates were used widely to sweeten soft drinks, ice creams and other processed foods. However, they are now thought to be carcinogenic and are banned in many countries, including Britain and USA.

Saccharin

Saccharin is the most common artificial sweetening agent used today. It is a constituent of coal tar and is estimated to be 400 times sweeter than refined sugars. It is used widely in the food processing industry because it contains fewer calories than other sweeteners and it is cheaper. It has been estimated that five pence worth of saccharin is equivalent in sweetening power to one pound's (£) worth of sugar.

Saccharin has also been linked to certain types of cancer and is banned in a number of countries.

Nutrition should always be a prime consideration in choosing foods but it is worth remembering that biscuits, cakes and puddings are usually eaten from preference rather than need, and rarely make a significant or vital contribution to our daily nutritional require-ments. In any case they should always be eaten as part of a well balanced diet. The fact that brown sugars contain more nutrients than white sugars is not a valid reason for including them in one's diet. Any benefit these nutrients may provide is far outweighed by the potential health risks.

Undoubtedly the best natural sweeteners to use are fresh fruit and berries. They contain natural fruit sugars, a range of vitamins and minerals and valuable fibre. Most of the sugar found in fruits is in the form of fructose. It is absorbed into the blood system in a different way to sucrose and is less likely to cause extreme fluctuations in blood sugar levels. The presence of large amounts of water and fibre is significant too, ensuring that the food cannot be eaten in excessive quantities, overconsumption being a significant factor in many of the degenerative illnesses prevalent today.

Be a little more wary when using dried fruits, honey, malt extract and molasses. They are very sweet tasting and can be used to make delicious cakes, puddings and desserts that will satisfy most people's sweet tooth. Although they contain many nutrients they are low in water and (with the exception of dried fruits) are also low in fibre. In all cases their natural sugar content is high, in excess of 50 per cent. While it is much better to use them in preference to refined sugars try to use them in moderation and in recipes containing high fibre ingredients such as wholewheat flour. This adds valuable bulk which acts as a safeguard against the common problems associated with eating concentrated and refined foods, notably overconsumption and obesity.

The recipe section of this book includes many delicious dishes which show how unnecessary it is to add refined sugars to foods. In many cases, rather than improving the taste of the food, sugar may actually mask its real flavour. Biscuits, cakes, puddings and desserts made from unrefined, naturally sweet ingredients not only look attractive and taste delicious but are also truly nutritious.

A Guide to Good Baking

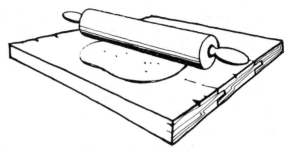

There are many methods of making cakes, pastries and biscuits and whichever method you use it is important to pay particular attention to the initial preparation. The appearance, flavour and texture of the finished product are dependent on the choice of ingredients, the care taken during mixing and the selection and preparation of a suitable baking tin or dish. I support the idea of adapting recipes to suit personal tastes, so by all means use raisins instead of sultanas but be careful not to alter the proportion of fat, flour and eggs as this can have disastrous effects upon the texture and consistency of the finished product.

When considering what to bake it may be necessary to take into account when the cake or pudding is to be eaten. Scones, for instance, must be eaten on the day they are baked and are actually at their very best when served warm and fresh from the oven. Biscuits and fruit cakes on the other hand will keep for several weeks in airtight containers and can be dipped into when needed. Similarly, some fruit desserts benefit from being chilled in a refrigerator for several hours before serving, while others need to be eaten straight away and any delay can result in them looking rather like a collapsed soufflé.

Cake Making

After baking, a perfect cake should be even in colour, well risen with a smooth, slightly rounded top. To ensure good results it is important to:

1 Measure the ingredients accurately.
2 Follow the recipe carefully.
3 Prepare the cake tin thoroughly, brushing it with oil and lining it with greaseproof paper as necessary.
4 Work quickly when using bicarbonate of soda and baking powder.
5 Introduce as much air as possible into the mixture, beating the eggs thoroughly and sifting the flour.
6 Bake at the correct temperature.

Although it is not always possible to produce consistently 'perfect' results, persistent failures are an indication of an error in the preparation of the cake.

Possible faults:

A cake sinking in the middle during or after baking may be due to too much raising agent, too cool an oven, too little flour or opening the oven door or moving the cake before it has become firm.

Fruit sinking to the bottom of the cake could be a result of the mixture being too soft, too much raising agent, using damp fruit or opening the oven door before the cake has become firm.

The top of the cake cracking during baking may be the result of using too small a cake tin, opening the oven door before the cake has become firm or not lining the cake tin adequately.

A dry cake that becomes stale quickly may be due to using too much raising agent, too little flour or eggs, making the mixture too stiff, cooking in too hot an oven or for too long a period.

A cake with a crumbly, open texture is more likely to result from insufficient creaming and careless mixing.

A heavy, solid cake may be a result of mixing the ingredients together for too long after the addition of the flour, using too much fat, making the mixture too thin or cooking at too low a temperature or for too short a time.

Pastry Making

Many sweet dishes are made with pastry and it is important to be able to make a pastry that tastes as good as it looks. There is no need to be wary about making pastry at home, as it really is quite easy.

General rules for making pastry:

1   When using wholewheat flour choose one that has been finely milled.
2   Keep all the ingredients cool and use cold water where necessary.
3   Introduce as much air as possible by holding the hands above the top of the bowl while rubbing the fat into the flour.
4   Roll out the pastry with short, quick movements.
5   Use a minimum amount of flour when rolling out the dough.
6   All pies and flans cooked in ceramic dishes should either be blind baked for 10 minutes or stood on a preheated baking tray when cooked with the filling.
7   Bake at the correct temperature.

Possible problems:

A hard, tough pastry may be the result of adding too much liquid or handling the dough too often.

A crumbly pastry may be the result of using too coarse a flour or using insufficient water.

A rubbery, greasy pastry may be due to too low an oven temperature.

Biscuit Making

Biscuits are quick and easy to prepare and will keep fresh and crisp for many weeks in an airtight tin. For every basic recipe there are a dozen variations that you can invent for yourself simply by altering the flavouring, shape and decoration.

Tips for making good biscuits:

1 Mix the ingredients together lightly, using the fingertips.
2 Roll the dough out thinly on a lightly floured board.
3 Cut the biscuits into even shapes and sizes.
4 Cut as many biscuits as possible from the first rolling.
5 Cook at the correct temperature.
6 Most biscuits should be cooled on a wire rack but softer varieties such as gingernuts are best left on the baking sheet for 5–10 minutes to firm up.

Possible faults:
Tough, leathery biscuits may be the result of over handling the dough or using too much flour when rolling out.

Soft biscuits may be the result of cooking for too short a time or at too low a temperature, not storing them in an airtight container or storing them with moist cakes.

Uneven browning may be due to using a high sided baking tray or cutting out the biscuits into different sizes.

Scone Making
A good scone should be well risen, light and golden brown.
Hints on successful scone making:

1 Handle the ingredients lightly.
2 Work quickly.
3 Introduce as much air into the mixture as possible, by sifting the flour and holding the hands above the bowl while mixing the ingredients together.
4 Roll out the dough to a thickness of 2.5 cm (1 inch).
5 Cut out as many scones as possible from the first rolling.
6 Bake immediately.

Reasons for failure:
Heavy, flat scones may be due to insufficient raising agent, working too slowly, rolling out the dough too thinly or cooking at an incorrect temperature.

Before beginning to prepare a dish for the first time read the recipe carefully and check that you have sufficient time and all the necessary ingredients. Decide whether to follow the metric, British imperial or US cup measurements and weigh out the ingredients before you begin baking. In case you are unfamiliar with any of the ingredients used in my recipes a comprehensive glossary has been included.

Most of the recipes specify wholewheat flour although unbleached white flour and soya flour are used in a number of dishes. Some people, accustomed to using wholewheat flour for making bread, are nonetheless a little cautious about using it in other ways. Really there is no need to worry, brown flour is just as easy to handle as white varieties, although I would suggest using a finely milled flour. After making wholewheat cakes and pastries several times you will probably find that you prefer their flavour and texture to those made with traditional white flours.

Ingredients

Agar Agar
A clear setting agent used to make jellies and fruit desserts.

Arrowroot
A fine white powder used as a thickening agent to make clear sauces and glazes.

Blind baking
A term used to describe the baking of a pastry case without a filling.

Carob flour
A flour made from the carob pod which tastes a little of cinnamon and chocolate. It is used to sweeten and flavour cakes, puddings, desserts etc.

Concentrated fruit juice
A sweet syrup. Choose a brand free from added sugars, preservatives, colour or flavouring agents.

Curd
A soured milk product. The liquid or whey is drained off to leave the solid curd.

Dried fruits
The majority of commercial dried fruit is sprayed with food grade mineral oil to prevent sticking and to give a moist appearance. Mineral oils, also called paraffin oils, prevent the body absorbing vitamins A, D E and K. Try to buy fruits that are untreated or coated in vegetable oils.

Dry roasting
Roasting food in the oven without any fat. The food can be cooked in a similar fashion in a pan on the stove top or under the grill. It is used mainly in the preparation of nuts, seeds and whole grains.

Kiwi fruit
Chinese gooseberry.

Low fat cream cheese
A low fat dairy product, also sold as quark.

Maize meal
A fine, yellow flour milled from maize. It is also known as corn meal.

Millet	A light, nutty grain.
Mugi miso	A high protein paste made from soya beans. It has a rich, mellow flavour and is used in sweet and savoury dishes.
Natural unsweetened fruit juice	Also sold as 'pure' fruit juice. Use fruit juices that are free from added sugars, preservatives, flavouring and colouring agents.
Oat flakes	Jumbo oats.
Oils	The best oils are labelled cold pressed, and retain the flavour and nutritional value of the fruit or seed from which they have been extracted. They may also be sold as 'unrefined' or 'virgin' oils.
Porridge oats	Rolled oats.
Sesame seeds	Small crunchy seeds. Gentle roasting brings out their delicious nutty flavour.
Shoyu soya sauce	A natural soya sauce. Some soya sauces are artificially manufactured, having an inferior nutritional value and containing many chemical additives.
Soya flour	A yellow flour made from soya beans. Unlike most other flours it is high in protein and low in carbohydrate.
Sugarless jam	A jam made from fresh or dried fruit and fruit juices. Such jams contain no refined sugars.
Tofu	Also known as soya bean curd. It is low in fat and high in protein and can be used in place of yoghurt, soft cheese and cream in many recipes.
Unbleached white flour	100 per cent wholewheat flour should normally be used in the kitchen. Occasionally, however, it is useful to have a lighter, refined flour for making some types of sauces and pastries. Choose an 'unbleached' variety that contains no additives or bleaching agents. Don't be surprised if it looks 'grubby' in comparison to its 'whiter than white' counterparts.
Whole wheat	Wheat groats or wheat berries.
Wholewheat flour	This is the best flour to use in terms of flavour, nutritional value and dietary fibre. As the name suggests, it contains every part of the whole wheat grain.

Wholewheat SR flour   Ideal for cakes and puddings. If unavailable use wholewheat flour (plain) and baking powder. 4 oz wholewheat flour plus 1 tsp baking powder is equal to 4 oz wholewheat SR flour.

Wholewheat semolina   A semolina containing fine bran flakes and wheatgerm. It has a sweeter, nuttier flavour than mass produced varieties.

Zest   The outer skin of citrus fruits containing the essential flavouring oils.

Cookery Terms

British and American Food Terms

British	American
baked/unbaked pastry case	baked/unbaked pie shell
baking tray	cookie sheet
bicarbonate of soda	baking soda
biscuits	cookies/crackers
biscuit mixture/dough	cookie dough
butter muslin	cheese cloth
cake mixture	cake batter
cake tin	cake pan
desiccated coconut	dried coconut
double cream	heavy/whipping cream
essence	extract
greaseproof paper	wax paper
green grapes	white grapes
grill/grilled	broil/broiled
knock back dough	punch down dough
low fat cream cheese	ricotta/diet cheese
maize flour	corn meal
millet	whole hulled millet
mixture or dough	batter
natural yoghurt	unflavoured yoghurt
porridge oats	rolled oats/quick cooking oats
pudding basin	ovenproof bowl
scones	biscuits
semolina	semolina flour
single cream	light coffee cream
sour cream	cultured sour cream
soya sauce	soy sauce
stoned	pitted
sultanas	seedless white raisins
top and tail goosberries	clean gooseberries
wholewheat plain flour	wholewheat all purpose flour
wholewheat SR flour	wholewheat all purpose flour sifted with baking powder
yeast, dried	active dry yeast
yeast, fresh	compressed yeast
zest	grated rind

Conversion Tables

British/American Conversion Tables

British	American
1 teaspoon (tsp), level	1 teaspoon, heaped
1 dessertspoon (dessertsp), level	1 dessertspoon, heaped
1 tablespoon (tbsp), level	1 tablespoon, heaped
8 fluid ounce (fl oz)	1 US cup
16 fluid ounce (fl oz)	1 US pint

Breakfast Foods, Bars and Biscuits

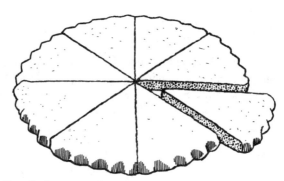

Muesli

Muesli is a very popular breakfast food and has superseded conventional cornflakes in many homes. It is highly nutritious and very filling. Prepacked muesli can be bought in most supermarkets and grocers but it is much more fun to make your own. Any type of dried fruit or nut can be used depending on personal taste, availability and cost. The choice of flakes, however, is more important and the inclusion of five different grains adds to the texture, flavour and nutritional value of the muesli.

Metric/Imperial	American
100 g/4 oz porridge oats	2 cups rolled oats
100 g/4 oz oat flakes	2 cups oat flakes
50 g/2 oz barley flakes	1 cup barley flakes
50 g/2 oz rye flakes	1 cup rye flakes
50 g/2 oz wheat flakes	1 cup wheat flakes
50 g/2 oz raisins	½ cup raisins
50 g/2 oz sultanas	½ cup white seedless raisins
50 g/2 oz hazelnuts, chopped	½ cup hazelnuts, chopped
50 g/2 oz sunflower seeds	½ cup sunflower seeds

Mix all the ingredients together in a large bowl. Serve with fresh fruit and milk.

Muesli can also be soaked overnight in a little water or fruit juice and served with chopped fruit and yoghurt.

Super Muesli

A moist and fruity breakfast cereal. It can be made in larger quantities and stored in a refrigerator for several days.

Metric/Imperial	American
60 ml/4 tbsps porridge oats	4 tbsps rolled oats
60 ml/4 tbsps oat flakes	4 tbsps oat flakes
120 ml/8 tbsps water	8 tbsps water
2 eating apples, grated	2 eating apples, grated
juice of 2 oranges	juice of 2 oranges
45 ml/3 tbsps ground almonds	3 tbsps ground almonds

Soak the porridge oats and oat flakes in the water overnight. Add the grated apples, the juice from the oranges and the ground almonds. Mix together well before serving.

Granola

A crunchy breakfast food that can be eaten on its own or mixed with muesli. It is so delicious that many people eat it as a snack in place of sweets, chocolates and biscuits.

Metric/Imperial	American
450 g/1 lb oat flakes	1 lb oat flakes
30 ml/2 tbsps sunflower oil	2 tbsps sunflower oil
50 g/2 oz sesame seeds	½ cup sesame seeds
50 g/2 oz desiccated coconut	1 cup dried coconut
50 g/2 oz hazelnuts, chopped	½ cup hazelnuts, chopped
a few drops of vanilla essence	a few drops of vanilla extract
100 g/4 oz raisins	¾ cup raisins

Preheat the oven to gas mark 5 (190°C/375°F).

Mix all the ingredients together in a large bowl *except* for the raisins. Place the mixture on a baking tray and cook for 20–25 minutes, turning the granola over several times to roast it evenly. When it is a golden colour remove from the oven and leave aside to cool. After it has cooled mix in the raisins.

Store in an airtight jar or container.

Frumenty

A hearty and nutritious breakfast food eaten in the north of England since the time of the Roman invasion. Traditionally the wheat was cooked overnight in a very slow oven with milk and spices. Eggs were beaten into the mixture just before it was served. My version of frumenty is lighter, fruitier and takes less time to prepare. It can be eaten piping hot on cold winter mornings or refreshingly chilled during the summer months.

Metric/Imperial	American
225 g/8 oz wheat berries	1½ cups wheat berries
850 ml/1½ pts water	3¼ cups water
675 g/1½ lbs cooking apples, cored	1½ lbs baking apples cored
275 ml/10 fl oz natural unsweetened apple juice	1¼ cups natural unsweetened apple juice
100 g/4 oz sultanas	¾ cup white seedless raisins
2.5 ml/½ tsp ground cinnamon	½ tsp ground cinnamon
2.5 ml/½ tsp ground nutmeg	½ tsp ground nutmeg

Dry roast the wheat berries in a pan until they begin to smell deliciously nutty. Remove from the heat and cool slightly before adding the water. Cover and bring to the boil. Simmer gently for 1½ hours until tender. Slice the apples and place in a pan with the apple juice and the remaining ingredients. Simmer gently for 5–10 minutes until the apples begin to soften. Drain the cooked wheat and stir into the apple mixture.

Serve hot or cold.

Apple Pancakes

A real treat for a leisurely, weekend breakfast.
This quantity makes ten pancakes.

Metric/Imperial	American
batter	*batter*
50 g/2 oz wholewheat flour	2 tbsps wholewheat flour
50 g/ 2 oz unbleached white flour	2 tbsps unbleached white flour
1 large egg, beaten	1 large egg, beaten
275 ml/10 fl oz milk	1¼ cups milk
pinch of salt	pinch of salt
soya oil for cooking	soy oil for cooking
filling	*filling*
450 g/1 lb eating apples, cored and sliced	1 lb eating apples, cored and sliced
50 g/2 oz raisins	½ cup raisins
pinch of ground cinnamon	pinch of ground cinnamon
pinch of ground cloves	pinch of ground cloves
pinch of ground nutmeg	pinch of ground nutmeg
2–3 drops of vanilla essence	2–3 drops of vanilla extract
45–60 ml/3–4 tbsps water	3–4 tbsps water

To make the batter mix the flour and salt
together in a bowl. Make a well in the centre
and add the beaten egg. Pour in half the liquid
and gradually work into the mixture. Mix well
until smooth. Add the remaining liquid a little
at a time, stirring constantly. Beat the batter
vigorously until frothy.

Place all the filling ingredients in a pan and
cook gently until the apples are tender and the
mixture is almost dry.

Heat a little soya oil in a frying pan, running
it over the bottom and around the sides of the
pan. Drain off any excess. Beat the batter again
before pouring 15 ml/1 tbsp (1 tbsp) of batter
into the fairly hot pan. Swirl the batter round to
coat the pan thinly but evenly. When the
underside of the pancake is patterned brown
and the surface has set, turn it over to cook the
other side. The second side always cooks a little
quicker and it may be necessary to turn the heat
down to prevent burning.

Spoon a little of the filling into the centre of
each pancake and roll it up. Arrange the
pancakes on a dish and keep them in a warm
oven until they are all ready to serve.

Date Square

Metric/Imperial
filling
225 g/8 oz dried dates,
pitted and chopped
200 ml/7 fl oz water
pinch of ground cinnamon
5 ml/1 tsp lemon zest

pastry
100 g/4 oz wholewheat
flour
100 g/4 oz wholewheat
semolina
125 g/4½ oz butter
30 ml/6 tsps cold water

to glaze
a little beaten egg

American
filling
2 cups dried dates, pitted
and chopped
1 cup water
pinch of ground cinnamon
1 tsp grated lemon rind

pastry
¾ cup wholewheat flour
1 cup wholewheat
semolina flour
½ cup butter
6 tsps cold water

to glaze
a little beaten egg

Preheat the oven to gas mark 5 (190°C/375°F).

To make the filling, put the dates and the water in a pan and cook gently for 5–10 minutes until they begin to soften. Stir in the cinnamon and lemon zest and leave to cool.

To make the pastry, mix the flour and semolina together in a bowl. Rub in the butter with the fingertips until the mixture resembles breadcrumbs. Add the water and press together lightly to form a pastry dough.

Divide the pastry in half and roll out two matching squares on a floured board. Place one piece of pastry on an oiled baking tray and cover with the date mixture, leaving a narrow margin round the edge. Lay the remaining pastry on the top, moisten the edges with a little water and pinch them together to seal. Trim away any surplus pastry and brush with the beaten egg. Bake for 20–25 minutes.

Leave to cool in the tin.

Glazed Apple and Apricot Slice

A delicious pastry filled with fresh and dried fruit. It can be eaten warm or cold.

Metric/Imperial
filling
150 g/5 oz dried apricots,
chopped
275 ml/10 fl oz water
2 Cox's eating apples,
cored

pastry
175 g/6 oz wholewheat
flour
5 ml/1 tsp baking
powder
90 g/3½ oz butter
30–35 ml/5–6 tsps milk

to glaze
a little beaten egg
15 g/½ oz butter

American
filling
1¼ cups dried apricots,
chopped
1¼ cups water
2 Cox's eating apples,
cored

pastry
1¼ cups wholewheat
flour
1 tsp baking powder
½ cup butter
5–6 tsps milk

to glaze
a little beaten egg
1 tbsp butter

Preheat the oven to gas mark 7 (220°C/425°F).

To make the filling, simmer the apricots and water together gently in a pan for 10 minutes. Slice the apples and add to the pan. Cook for a further 10–15 minutes until both fruits are soft. Mix together lightly with a fork and leave aside to cool.

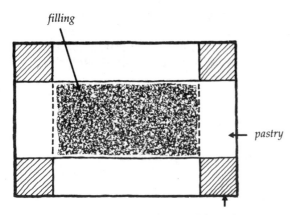

filling

pastry

cut out corners and discard

To make the pastry, combine the flour and baking powder in a bowl. Rub in the butter with the fingertips until the mixture resembles breadcrumbs. Add sufficient milk to form a smooth firm dough. Roll out on a floured board to form a rectangle measuring 20cm × 30cm (8 ins × 12 ins) and place on a greased baking tray.

Spread the cooked fruit over the pastry leaving a 5cm (2 ins) margin around the edge. Fold over the short pastry ends. Trim the corners to a single thickness. Make a series of cuts, 3.75cm (1½ ins) at an angle of 45° and at an interval of 2.5cm (1 in) in the pastry along both sides of the filling. Be careful not to cut through the outer edges. Fold the two sides over the filling so that they meet in the middle. Pinch together to seal. Brush with beaten egg and sprinkle with the flaked almonds. Bake for 25 minutes.

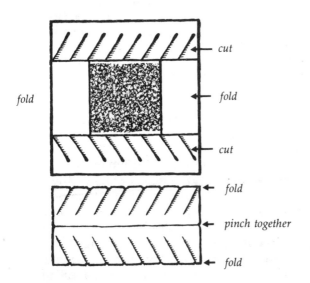

cut

fold

fold

cut

fold

pinch together

fold

Wholewheat Éclairs with Cream Cheese and Pear Filling

Metric/Imperial	American
filling	*filling*
100 g/4 oz dried pears, chopped	1 cup dried pears, chopped
275 ml/10 fl oz water	1¼ cups water
100 g/4 oz low fat cream cheese	½ cup ricotta/diet cheese
pastry	*pastry*
50 g/2 oz butter	¼ cup butter
150 ml/5 fl oz water	½ cup water
75 g/2½ oz wholewheat flour	½ cup wholewheat flour
2 eggs, beaten	2 eggs, beaten

Soak the pears in the water overnight.

Preheat the oven to gas mark 7 (220°C/425°F).

To make the pastry melt the butter with the water in a pan. Bring to the boil. Remove from the heat and add the flour. Beat well until the mixture is smooth. Leave to cool slightly before gradually adding the eggs. Beat well until the pastry is smooth and shiny. Spoon into a piping bag with a plain round 1.5cm/½ ins nozzle. Pipe 7.5cm/3 ins strips of pastry onto a large, oiled baking tray. Bake for 20 minutes.

Reduce the oven temperature to gas mark 5(190°C/375°F).

Slit each éclair down one side to allow the steam to escape and return to the oven for a further 10 minutes until firm to touch. Leave to cool on a wire rack.

Put the soaked pears and their liquid in a pan and bring to the boil. Simmer gently until almost all of the water has evaporated away. Liquidize. Reserve a little of the fruit purée to glaze the top of the éclairs. Beat the cream cheese into the remaining fruit purée. Fill each éclair with a little fruit cream. Brush with the fruit glaze.

Sponge Fig Fingers

Metric/Imperial	American
175 g/6 oz dried figs, chopped	1½ cups dried figs, chopped
240 ml/8–9 fl oz milk	1 cup milk
5 ml/1 tsp vinegar	1 tsp vinegar
225 g/8 oz wholewheat flour	1½ cups wholewheat flour
10 ml/2 tsps bicarbonate of soda	2 tsps baking soda
2.5 ml/½ tsp ground cinnamon	½ tsp ground cinnamon
2.5 ml/½ tsp ground ginger	½ tsp ground ginger
100 g/4 oz butter	½ cup butter

Pre–heat the oven to gas mark 5 (190°C/375°F).

Put the figs and milk in a pan and bring to the boil. Leave to cool for 10–15 minutes. Add the vinegar and blend until smooth. Mix the flour, bicarbonate of soda, ground cinnamon and ground ginger together in a bowl. Rub in the butter until it resembles breadcrumbs. Stir in the blended ingredients and mix together well. Spoon the fairly stiff mixture into an oiled and lined 17.5cm/7 ins square sandwich tin and bake for 20–25 minutes until golden brown and firm to touch.

Leave to cool for 10 minutes before turning out onto a wire rack. Cut into bars when cold.

Crunch

Metric/Imperial	American
225 g/8 oz butter	1 cup butter
75 ml/5 tbsps honey	5 tbsps honey
175 g/6 oz porridge oats	3 cups rolled oats
175 g/6 oz wholewheat flour	1¼ cups wholewheat flour
10 ml/2 level tsps ground ginger	2 tsps ground ginger

Preheat the oven to gas mark 4 (180°C/350°F).

Put the butter and honey in a pan and heat gently until melted. Stir in the remaining ingredients. Spread the mixture in a shallow, oiled tin and bake for 15–20 minutes.

Mark into squares while warm, but leave to cool and firm up in the tin.

Mint Pastie

An unusual recipe that is very popular in the north of England. It consists of a pastry case filled with succulent, sweet currants and fresh mint.

Metric/Imperial	American
filling	*filling*
225 g/8 oz currants	1½ cups currants
90 ml/6 tbsps natural unsweetened apple juice	6 tbsps natural unsweetened apple juice
8–10 sprigs of fresh mint, chopped	8–10 sprigs of fresh mint, chopped
pastry	*pastry*
225 g/8 oz wholewheat flour	1½ cups wholewheat flour
75 g/3 oz butter	a scant ½ cup butter
45 ml/3 tbsps soya oil	3 tbsps soy oil
35–40 ml/7–8 tsps cold water	7–8 tsps cold water
to glaze	*to glaze*
a little beaten egg	a little beaten egg

Preheat the oven to gas mark 6 (200°C/400°F).

Put the currants and apple juice in a pan and cook gently until most of the liquid has evaporated. Add the chopped mint. Leave aside.

To make the pastry, rub the butter and oil into the flour until the mixture resembles breadcrumbs. Add the water and lightly press the ingredients together with the fingertips to form a dough.

Divide the dough in half and roll out two

matching squares of pastry. Place one piece on an oiled baking tray and spoon over the currant mixture, leaving a narrow margin around the edge. Lay the remaining pastry over the top. Moisten the edges with a little water and press together to seal. Trim away any surplus pastry, brush with a little beaten egg and bake for 25 minutes.

Leave to cool in the tin.

Malty Flapjack

A sweet, chewy fruit bar that is a favourite with all children.

Metric/Imperial	American
100 g/4 oz butter	½ cup butter
45 ml/3 level tbsps malt extract	3 tbsps malt extract
60 ml/4 tbsps soya oil	4 tbsps soy oil
225 g/8 oz porridge oats	4 cups rolled oats
50 g/2 oz sultanas	½ cup white seedless raisins

Preheat the oven to gas mark 4 (180°C/350°F).

Heat the butter and malt extract together in a pan until melted. Add the remaining ingredients. Spread the mixture into a shallow, oiled tin and bake for 15–20 minutes.

Mark into squares while the flapjack is warm but leave to cool and firm up in the tin.

Orange and Sultana Scones

Scones are quick and easy to prepare but they do not keep and are best eaten on the day of baking. This quantity makes six to eight scones.

Metric/Imperial	American
225 g/8 oz wholewheat SR flour	1½ cups wholewheat flour sifted with baking powder
1.25 ml/¼ tsp bicarbonate of soda	¼ tsp baking soda
50 g/2 oz butter	¼ cup butter
100 g/4 oz sultanas	¾ cup white seedless raisins
75 ml/2½ fl oz natural unsweetened orange juice	5 tbsps natural unsweetened orange juice
75 ml/2½ fl oz milk	5 tbsps milk
5 ml/1 tsp orange zest	1 tsp grated orange rind
to glaze	*to glaze*
a little beaten egg	a little beaten egg

Preheat the oven to gas mark 6 (200°C/400°F).

Place the flour and bicarbonate of soda in a bowl and rub in the butter until the mixture resembles breadcrumbs. Add the remaining ingredients and press together with the fingertips to form a dough. Turn onto a floured board and knead lightly. Roll out to a thickness of 2.5cm (1 in) and cut into rounds. Place on a floured baking tray and brush with a little beaten egg. Bake for 15–20 minutes until well risen and golden.

Buttermilk and Date Scones

Buttermilk is a delicious low calorie low fat dairy product. It is, as the name suggests, a residue of butter making and when fresh has a frothy, slightly acid quality. Most of the buttermilk available in the shops is made from skimmed milk and a culture. It is slightly thicker and sharper than the genuine product but it can be used successfully in baking. Buttermilk is a traditional ingredient in soda bread and scones as it acts with the raising agents to make them light and well risen. This quantity makes six to eight scones.

Metric/Imperial	American
225 g/8 oz wholewheat flour	1½ cups wholewheat flour
1.25 ml/¼ tsp salt	¼ tsp salt
2.5 ml/½ tsp bicarbonate of soda	½ tsp baking soda
2.5 ml/½ tsp cream of tartar	½ tsp cream of tartar
25 g/1 oz butter	2 tbsps butter
75 g/3 oz dried dates, pitted and chopped	¾ cup dried dates, pitted and chopped
150 ml/5 fl oz buttermilk	½ cup buttermilk

Preheat the oven to gas mark 7 (220°C/425°F).

Mix the flour, salt, bicarbonate of soda and cream of tartar together in a bowl. Rub in the butter with the fingertips until the mixture resembles breadcrumbs. Add the chopped dates. Pour in the buttermilk and mix quickly to form a soft dough. Turn onto a floured board, knead lightly and roll out to a thickness of 2.5cm (1 in). Cut into rounds and bake on a lightly floured baking sheet for 15 minutes until golden brown.

Apple and Hazelnut Ring

Metric/Imperial	American
filling	*filling*
450 g/1 lb eating apples, peeled, cored and chopped	1 lb eating apples, peeled, cored and chopped
50 g/2 oz roasted hazelnuts, chopped	½ cup roasted hazelnuts, chopped
50 g/2 oz sultanas	½ cup white seedless raisins
1.25 ml/¼ tsp ground ginger	¼ tsp ground ginger
1.25 ml/¼ tsp grated nutmeg	¼ tsp grated nutmeg
5 ml/1 tsp lemon zest	1 tsp grated lemon rind
pastry	*pastry*
225 g/8 oz wholewheat SR flour	1½ cups wholewheat flour sifted with baking powder
115 g/4½ oz butter	½ cup butter
75–90 ml/5–7 tbsps cold water	5–7 tbsps cold water
to glaze	*to glaze*
a little beaten egg	a little beaten egg

Preheat the oven to gas mark 6 (200°C/400°F).

Place all the filling ingredients in a bowl and mix together.

To make the pastry, grate the butter into the flour and add sufficient water to make a fairly stiff dough. Roll out on a floured board to form an oblong 20cm × 40cm (8 ins × 16 ins).

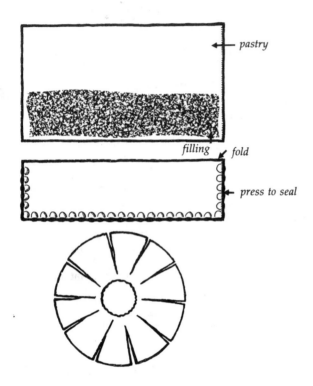

Carefully lift the pastry onto an oiled baking tray.

Spoon the filling lengthways over half of the pastry, leaving a margin around the edge. Fold the uncovered pastry over the filling, moisten the edges with water and pinch together to seal. Trim away any surplus pastry. Make a series of cuts in the pastry, 5cm (2 ins) apart, and carefully twist the roll to form a ring. Brush with the beaten egg and bake for 30–35 minutes.

Apple Jalousie

Jalousie is a word of French derivation, meaning a slatted shutter or venetian blind — hardly a word that would naturally spring to mind when describing a favourite recipe! But jalousie is a classic cookery term indicating the appearance of a dish rather than its ingredients. Apple jalousie is a light puff pastry crust attractively shaped and glazed and filled with sweet apples and sultanas.

Metric/Imperial	American
pastry	*pastry*
225 g/8 oz wholewheat flour	1½ cups wholewheat flour
225 g/8 oz butter	1 cup butter
5 ml/1 tsp lemon juice	1 tsp lemon juice
150 ml/5 fl oz cold water	½ cup cold water
filling	*filling*
450 g/1 lb Cox's eating apples, cored	1 lb Cox's eating apples, cored
50 g/2 oz sultanas	½ cup white seedless raisins
30 ml/2 tbsps sugarless apricot jam	2 tbsps sugarless apricot jam
to glaze	*to glaze*
15 ml/1 tbsp sugarless apricot jam	1 tbsp sugarless apricot jam
15 ml/1 tbsp water	1 tbsp water

To make wholewheat puff pastry, first put the flour in a mixing bowl and rub in a piece of butter the size of a walnut. Add the lemon juice and two thirds of the water. Mix together well and when the dough is beginning to form add the remaining water. Turn onto a floured board and knead for 2–3 minutes. Roll out into a square 2.25cm (¾ in) thick. Soften the butter and place it in the centre of the square. Fold over the sides of the square to enclose the butter. Wrap in greaseproof paper and chill for 30 minutes. Place on a floured board, seams uppermost, and flatten in several places with a rolling pin. Roll out into a rectangle 2.25cm (¾ in) thick. Divide the dough into three equal parts and fold the ends into the middle. Press the edges together to seal and turn the dough through 90°. Chill for 15 minutes. Repeat the rolling out, folding and chilling twice more.

Preheat the oven to gas mark 7 (220°C/425°F).

Roll out the pastry to a rectangle 0.75cm (¼ in) thick. Cut out a rectangle measuring 25cm × 10cm (10 ins × 4 ins) and fold in half

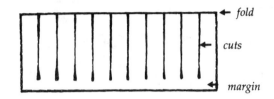

fold
cuts
margin

similar sized rectangle and place it on a dampened baking tray. Brush with the 30 ml (2 tbsps) sugarless apricot jam. Slice the apples and arrange them on top of the pastry, leaving a margin around the edge. Scatter the sultanas over the fruit. Dampen the pastry edges with a little water and carefully lift the folded pastry over the fruit, with the folded edge along the centre. Open out the rectangle and press the

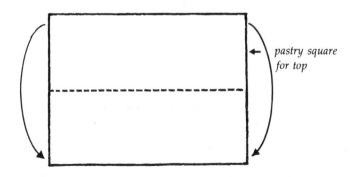

pastry square for top

lengthways. Cut across the fold at 0.75cm (¼ in) intervals, leaving a narrow margin around the edge. Use the remaining pastry to roll out a

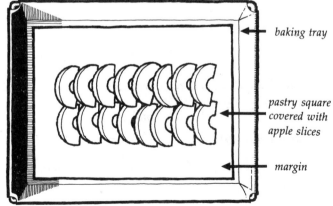

baking tray
pastry square covered with apple slices
margin

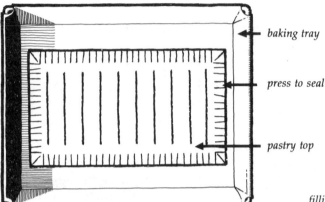

baking tray

press to seal

pastry top

edges together to seal. Chill the jalousie for 10 minutes and bake for 25 minutes.

Blend the remaining apricot jam and water together to make a glaze and brush over the crust. Return to the oven for 5–10 minutes until golden. Slide onto a wire rack and leave to cool.

Mince Pies

A delicious mincemeat filling that will appeal to vegetarians and non-vegetarians alike. Light, moist and fruity, these mince pies make a pleasant change to richer Christmas foods. This quantity makes twelve small pies.

Metric/Imperial	American
pastry	*pastry*
200 g/7 oz wholewheat flour	1½ cups wholewheat flour
150 g/5 oz butter	a scant ¾ cup butter
a squeeze of lemon juice	a squeeze of lemon juice
90–105 ml/6–7 tbsps cold water	6–7 tbsps cold water

filling
225 g/8 oz cooking apples, cored
1 medium sweet orange, peeled
50 g/2 oz carrot, finely grated
75 g/3 oz mixed dried fruit
150 ml/5 fl oz natural unsweetened apple juice
5 ml/1 tsp mugi miso
5 ml/1 tsp ground mixed spice

to glaze
a little beaten egg

filling
½ lb baking apples cored
1 medium sweet orange, peeled
½ cup carrot, finely grated
½ cup mixed dried fruit
½ cup natural unsweetened apple juice
1 tsp mugi miso
1 tsp ground mixed spice

to glaze
a little beaten egg

Preheat the oven to gas mark 6 (200°C/400°F).

To make the wholewheat flaky pastry, sift the flour into a large mixing bowl. Soften the butter with a knife and divide into four pieces. Rub one piece of fat into the flour. Add the lemon juice and water and mix to form a soft dough.

Roll out on a floured board to form a rectangle three times as long as it is wide. Using the second portion of butter, cover two thirds of the dough with evenly spaced dabs of fat. Fold the ends of the dough into the centre, making sure that the unbuttered section is in the middle. Seal the edges and turn the dough through 90°. Repeat the rolling, buttering and folding twice more. Wrap in greaseproof paper and chill for 30 minutes.

To make the filling, chop the apples and orange and put into a pan with the carrot, mixed dried fruit and apple juice. Simmer gently for 10 minutes until the apples soften. Blend the miso with a little of the liquid from the pan before adding to the cooked fruit. Stir in the spices and leave to cool.

Roll out the pastry on a lightly floured board, cut out twelve rounds and place in an oiled bun tin. Fill with a spoonful of the mincemeat. Cut out twelve smaller rounds and dampen their edges before putting them on top of the pies. Pinch the pastry edges together to seal, and brush with a little beaten egg. Bake for 20–25 minutes. Cool slightly in the tin before placing on a wire rack.

Wholewheat flaky pastry has a texture that 'melts in the mouth'. It is, however, time consuming to prepare. As Christmas is one of the busiest times of the year for the cook the idea of making flaky pastry may not seem particularly attractive. I would suggest that harassed and weary cooks make mince pies with ordinary (shortcrust) pastry which is easier and quicker to prepare.

Walnut Biscuits

Homemade biscuits are cheap and easy to bake and will keep well in airtight containers. Honey is used as a sweetening agent and to provide a good texture. Strong tasting honeys will also add to the flavour of the biscuit. This quantity makes fifteen biscuits.

Metric/Imperial	American
50 g/2 oz butter	¼ cup butter
30 ml/2 tbsps honey	2 tbsps honey
1 large egg, beaten	1 large egg, beaten
175 g/6 oz wholewheat flour	1¼ cups wholewheat flour
5 ml/1 level tsp baking powder	1 tsp baking powder
50 g/2 oz walnuts, chopped	½ cup walnuts, chopped
5 ml/1 tsp almond essence	1 tsp almond extract

Preheat the oven to gas mark 4 (180°C/350°F).

Heat the butter and honey together gently in a pan until melted. Leave the mixture to become tepid before adding the beaten egg. Mix the wholewheat flour and baking powder together and stir into the mixture. Add the walnuts and almond essence and press together with the fingertips to form a soft dough. Shape into small balls using 15 ml (1 tbsp) of the mixture. Place on an oiled baking sheet and flatten the biscuits by pressing down lightly with a palette knife. Bake for 15–20 minutes.

Cool on a wire rack.

Fruit Shrewsbury Biscuits

This quantity makes twenty biscuits.

Metric/Imperial	American
100 g/4 oz butter	½ cup butter
1 large egg	1 large egg
60 ml/4 level tbsps clear honey	4 tbsps clear honey
250 g/9 oz wholewheat flour	1¾ cups wholewheat flour
50 g/2 oz raisins	½ cup raisins

Preheat the oven to gas mark 5 (190°C/375°F).

Soften the butter and blend together with the egg and honey. When smooth and creamy pour into a mixing bowl and fold in the flour. Add the raisins. Press together with the fingertips to form a dough. Roll out on a lightly floured board and cut into rounds. Place on an oiled baking tray and cook for 15 minutes.

Cool on a wire rack.

Orange Biscuits

This quantity makes twenty biscuits.

Metric/Imperial	American
75 ml/5 tbsps concentrated orange juice	5 tbsps concentrated orange juice
90 ml/6 tbsps soya oil	6 tbsps soy oil
1 large egg	1 large egg
275 g/10 oz wholewheat flour	2 cups wholewheat flour
100 g/4 oz sultanas	¾ cup white seedless raisins
5–10 ml/1–2 tsps orange zest	1–2 tsps grated orange rind

Preheat the oven to gas mark 5 (190°C/375°F).

Beat the concentrated orange juice, soya oil and egg together. Add the remaining ingredients and mix well. Press together with the fingertips to form a dough. Turn onto a floured board and roll out thinly. Cut into rounds and place on an oiled baking tray and cook for 15 minutes.

Cool on a wire rack.

Gingernuts

A lightly spiced, chewy biscuit that is especially easy to bake. This quantity makes sixteen biscuits.

Metric/Imperial	American
100 g/4 oz wholewheat SR flour	¾ cup wholewheat flour sifted with baking powder
5 ml/1 level tsp bicarbonate of soda	1 tsp baking soda
5 ml/1 rounded tsp ground ginger	1 tsp ground ginger
50 g/2 oz butter	¼ cup butter
30 ml/2 rounded tbsps clear honey	2 tbsps clear honey

Preheat the oven to gas mark 5 (190°C/375°F).

Mix the flour, bicarbonate of soda and ground ginger together in a bowl. Rub in the butter until the mixture resembles breadcrumbs. Add the honey and mix together with the fingertips to form a soft dough. Divide the mixture into four and four again. Roll into sixteen small balls and place them, well apart, on an oiled baking tray. Flatten the balls slightly and bake for 15 minutes until golden coloured.

Leave on the baking tray for 5–10 minutes to firm up before removing to a wire cooling rack.

Melting Peanut Cookies

This quantity makes ten to twelve biscuits.

Metric/Imperial	American
125 g/5 oz wholewheat SR flour	1 cup wholewheat flour sifted with baking powder
25 g/1 oz butter	2 tbsps butter
45 ml/3 tbsps corn germ oil	3 tbsps corn germ oil
50 g/ 2 oz crunchy peanut butter	a scant ¼ cup crunchy peanut butter
30 ml/2 tbsps concentrated apple juice	2 tbsps concentrated apple juice
30 ml/2 tbsps sesame seeds	2 tbsps sesame seeds

Preheat the oven to gas mark 4 (180°C/350°F).

Put the flour in a mixing bowl and rub in the butter and oil. Add the peanut butter and concentrated apple juice and press together lightly with the fingertips to form a dough. Roll out thinly on a floured board, sprinkle with the sesame seeds and run the rolling pin lightly over the surface. Cut into rounds and place on an oiled baking tray. Bake for 12–15 minutes.

Leave to cool on the baking tray for 5 minutes before placing on a wire cooling rack.

Cakes and Tea Breads

Honeyed Sultana Cake

A delicious honey flavoured cake that is popular with everyone.

Metric/Imperial	American
100 g/4 oz butter	½ cup butter
45 ml/3 tbsps clear honey	3 tbsps clear honey
2 medium eggs	2 medium eggs
275 g/10 oz wholewheat SR flour	2 cups wholewheat flour sifted with baking powder
100 g/4 oz sultanas	¾ cup white seedless raisins
45 ml/3 tbsps milk	3 tbsps milk

Preheat the oven to gas mark 4 (180°C/350°F).

Cut the butter into walnut sized pieces and blend with the honey and eggs. Put the flour into a bowl and fold in the blended ingredients. Mix in the sultanas and the milk. Spoon the cake mixture into an oiled cake, 17.5 cm (7 ins) tin, making a small hollow in the centre. Bake for 1–1¼ hours.

Leave to cool in the tin for 10 minutes before turning out onto a wire cooling rack.

Butterfly Buns

I used to enjoy baking these buns when I was small. They were called butterfly buns by my family because two pieces of bun are arranged on the top of the creamed filling to resemble the wings of a butterfly. This quantity makes twelve buns.

Metric/Imperial	American
150 g/5 oz wholewheat SR flour	1 cup wholewheat SR flour
25 g/ 1 oz carob flour	2 tbsps carob flour
75 g/3 oz butter	a scant ½ cup butter
45 ml/3 tbsps honey	3 tbsps honey
2 medium eggs, beaten	2 medium eggs, beaten
15–30 ml/1–2 tbsps milk	1–2 tbsps milk

filling	*filling*
100 g/4 oz butter	½ cup butter
50 g/2 oz carob flour	4 tbsps carob flour
a few drops of vanilla essence	a few drops of vanilla extract
15 ml/1 tbsp warm water	1 tbsp warm water

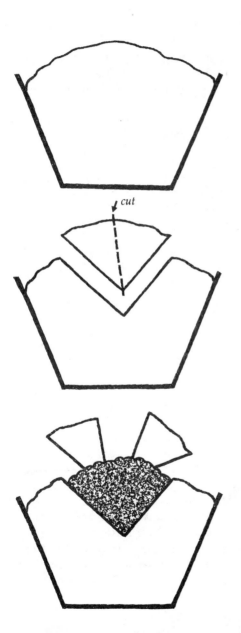

cut

Preheat the oven to gas mark 4 (180°C/350°F).

Combine the wholewheat SR flour and carob flour in a bowl. Melt the butter and honey together in a pan and gradually stir in to the flours. Add the milk and eggs and beat well until smooth. Spoon the mixture into paper bun cases, place in a bun tin and bake for 20 minutes.

When cool cut out the centre of each bun with a small pointed knife, being careful not to cut through the bottom.

To make the filling, put the butter in a bowl and cream until soft and smooth. Gradually beat in the carob flour, vanilla essence and water until stiff and creamy. Fill the hollowed out buns with the butter cream. Cut the conical piece of cake, removed from the centre of each bun, into two halves, from top to bottom. Press the two halves into the cream filling to form the wings of the butterfly.

Carob Fruit Cake

A dark, rich fruit cake sweetened with plump raisins and natural orange juice and flavoured with carob.

Metric/Imperial	American
450 g/1 lb raisins	1 lb raisins
275 ml/10 fl oz natural unsweetened orange juice	1¼ cups natural unsweetened orange juice
175 g/6 oz butter, softened	¾ cup butter, softened
3 medium eggs	3 medium eggs
250 g/9 oz wholewheat flour	1¾ cups wholewheat flour
75 g/3 oz carob flour	1 cup carob flour
10 ml/2 tsps baking powder	2 tsps baking powder
grated rind of 2 medium oranges	grated rind of 2 medium oranges

Soak the raisins in the orange juice overnight.

Preheat the oven to gas mark 4 (180°C/350°F).

Blend the butter and the eggs together until smooth and creamy. Mix the wholewheat flour, carob flour and baking powder together in a bowl and gradually fold in the blended ingredients. Add the soaked raisins, their juice and the orange zest. Spoon the cake mixture into an oiled and lined cake tin 17.5cm (7 ins) and bake for 1 hour. Reduce the oven temperature to gas mark 3 (160°C/325°F) and bake for a further 1¼ hours.

Leave to cool for 15 minutes in the tin before placing on a wire cooling rack.

Banana Bread

A sweet, moist sponge cake, full of the goodness and flavour of bananas and attractively topped with glazed apple slices.

Metric/Imperial	American
175 g/6 oz ripe bananas, peeled	1 cup ripe bananas, peeled
2 medium eggs	2 medium eggs
3 drops of vanilla essence	3 drops of vanilla extract
100 g/4 oz butter	½ cup butter
15 ml/1 tbsp honey	1 tbsp honey
150 g/5 oz wholewheat flour	1 cup wholewheat flour
25 g/1 oz desiccated coconut	½ cup dried coconut
10 ml/2 level tsps baking powder	2 tsps baking powder
1 red eating apple	1 red eating apple
to glaze	*to glaze*
15 ml/1 tbsp honey	1 tbsp honey
15 ml/1 tbsp hot water	1 tbsp hot water

Preheat the oven to gas mark 4 (180°C/350°F).

Blend the bananas, eggs and vanilla essence together until smooth and creamy. Gently melt the butter and honey together in a pan and when tepid stir in the blended ingredients. Combine the wholewheat flour, coconut and baking powder in a bowl and gradually fold in the wet ingredients. Pour into an oiled and lined 20cm (8 ins) square sandwich tin. Core and slice the apple and arrange the slices on top of the mixture. Bake for 25–30 minutes.

To make the glaze dissolve the honey in the hot water and brush over the freshly baked, warm cake. Leave to cool in the tin for 10 minutes before turning out onto a wire cooling rack.

Carrot Cake

The carrot cake originated in the USA but is now popular on both sides of the Atlantic. Carrots are surprisingly sweet and can be used successfully in a variety of dishes. Here they are combined with dates and spices to make a delicious, moist and spicy cake.

Metric/Imperial	American
75 g/3 oz dried dates, pitted and chopped	¾ cup dried dates, pitted and chopped
70 ml/2½ fl oz water	5 tbsps water
100 g/4 oz butter	½ cup butter
2 medium eggs	2 medium eggs
150 g/5 oz wholewheat SR flour	1 cup wholewheat flour sifted with baking powder
100 g/4 oz carrot, finely grated	1 cup carrot, finely grated
25 g/1 oz ground almonds	¼ cup ground almonds
15 ml/1 tbsp milk	1 tbsp milk
grated rind of 1 large orange	grated rind of 1 large orange
2.5 ml/½ tsp ground ginger	½ tsp ground ginger
2.5 ml/½ tsp ground cinnamon	½ tsp ground cinnamon
2.5 ml/½ tsp ground mixed spice	½ tsp ground mixed spice

Preheat the oven to gas mark 4 (180°C/350°F).

Cook the dates in the water gently for 10 minutes until soft. Blend the dates, cooking liquid, softened butter and eggs together until light and creamy. Fold in the remaining ingredients. Place the mixture in an oiled and lined 17.5cm (7 ins) cake tin and bake for 50–60 minutes.

Leave to cool in the tin for 5 minutes before turning out onto a wire cooling rack.

Carob Sponge Cake

Metric/Imperial	American
250 g/9 oz wholewheat flour	1¾ cups wholewheat flour
40 g/1½ oz carob flour	3 tbsps carob flour
5 ml/1 rounded tsp baking powder	1 tsp baking powder
100 g/4 oz butter	½ cup butter
15 ml/1 tbsp corn oil	1 tbsp corn oil
45 ml/3 tbsps honey	3 tbsps honey
3 medium eggs, beaten	3 medium eggs, beaten
filling	*filling*
100 g/4 oz low fat cream cheese	½ cup ricotta/diet cheese
15 ml/1 tbsp natural yoghurt	1 tbsp unflavoured yoghurt
15 ml/1 tbsp clear honey	1 tbsp clear honey

Preheat the oven to gas mark 4 (180°C/350°F).

Mix the wholewheat flour, carob flour and baking powder together in a bowl. Place the butter, oil and honey in a pan and heat gently until melted. Cool slightly before stirring into the dry ingredients. Add the eggs and beat well until the mixture has the consistency of thick cream. Pour into two oiled 15cm (6 ins) sandwich cake tins and bake for 25 minutes until firm to touch. Turn out onto a wire cooling rack.

To make the filling, blend the cheese, yoghurt and honey together until smooth and creamy. When the cake is cold spread the filling over the base of one of the cakes and sandwich the two pieces together.

Carob and Raisin Loaf

Metric/Imperial	American
175 g/6 oz raisins	1 cup raisins
150 ml/5 fl oz milk	½ cup milk
50 g/2 oz butter	¼ cup butter
2 large eggs	2 large eggs
60 ml/4 tbsps sunflower oil	4 tbsps sunflower oil
150 g/5 oz wholewheat SR flour	1 cup wholewheat flour sifted with baking powder
25 g/1 oz carob flour	2 tbsps carob flour
50 g/2 oz porridge oats	1 cup rolled oats

Preheat the oven to gas mark 4 (180°C/350°F).

Blend the raisins, milk, butter, eggs and oil together until smooth and creamy. Mix the wholewheat flour, carob flour and oats together in a bowl. Stir in the blended mixture. Spoon into an oiled and lined 900 g/2 lb loaf tin and bake for 1 hour.

Ginger Cake

This cake is loosely based on an old recipe for a 'trench cake' popular during the First World War.

Metric/Imperial	American
175 g/6 oz dried dates, pitted and chopped	1½ cup dried dates, pitted and chopped
250 ml/9 fl oz milk	1 cup milk
5 ml/1 tsp vinegar	1 tsp vinegar
225 g/8 oz wholewheat flour	1½ cups wholewheat flour
10 ml/2 tsps bicarbonate of soda	2 tsps baking soda
5 ml/1 tsp ground ginger	1 tsp ground ginger
2.5 ml/½ tsp ground nutmeg	½ tsp ground nutmeg
100 g/4 oz butter	½ cup butter

Preheat the oven to gas mark 5 (190°C/375°F).

Put the dates and milk together in a pan and bring to the boil. Leave aside for 10 minutes. Add the vinegar and blend until smooth. Mix the dry ingredients together in a bowl and rub in the butter until the mixture resembles breadcrumbs. Stir in the blended ingredients. Spoon the fairly stiff mixture into an oiled and lined 900 g/2 lb loaf tin. Bake for 1–1¼ hours.

Old Fashioned Parkin

A sticky gingerbread, the texture and flavour of which improve with age.

Metric/Imperial	American
175 g/6 oz butter	¾ cup butter
45 ml/3 tbsps honey	3 tbsps honey
30 ml/2 tbsps molasses	2 tbsps molasses
275 ml/10 fl oz milk	1¼ cups milk
3 medium eggs, beaten	3 medium eggs, beaten
5 ml/1 tsp bicarbonate of soda	1 tsp baking soda
15 ml/1 tbsp hot water	1 tbsp hot water
225 g/8 oz wholewheat flour	1½ cups wholewheat flour
100 g/4 oz porridge oats	2 cups rolled oats
10–15 ml/2–3 tsps ground ginger	2–3 tsps ground ginger
5 ml/1 tsp ground cinnamon	1 tsp ground cinnamon

Preheat the oven to gas mark 2 (150°C/300°F).

Place the butter, honey and molasses in a large pan and heat gently until melted. Stir in the milk and the beaten eggs. Dissolve the bicarbonate of soda in the hot water and add to the wet ingredients. Mix the flour, porridge oats, ginger and cinnamon together and add to the mixture. Beat well before pouring into an oiled and lined 20cm (8 ins) square cake tin. Bake for 1¼–1½ hours until firm to touch.

Cool in the tin.

Honey Cake

A delicious honey flavoured sponge cake.

Metric/Imperial	American
40 g/1½ oz butter	3 tbsps butter
60 ml/4 tbsp honey	4 tbsps honey
150 ml/5 fl oz milk	½ cup milk
200 g/7 oz wholewheat flour	1¼ cups wholewheat flour
10 ml/2 tsps baking powder	2 tsps baking powder
1 medium egg, beaten	1 medium egg, beaten

Preheat the oven to gas mark 6 (200°C/400°F).

Gently heat the butter and honey together until melted. Remove from the heat and add the milk. Combine the wholewheat flour and baking powder in a bowl. Mix in the melted butter, honey and milk and the beaten egg. Spoon the mixture into an oiled 17.5cm (7 ins) cake tin and bake for 25–30 minutes until well risen and golden brown.

Fruit Cake

An everyday fruit cake.

Metric/Imperial	American
225 g/8 oz mixed dried fruit	1½ cups mixed dried fruit
275 ml/10 fl oz natural unsweetened orange juice	1¼ cups natural unsweetened orange juice
225 g/8 oz wholewheat SR flour	1½ cups wholewheat flour sifted with baking powder
75 g/3 oz butter	a scant ½ cup butter
2 large eggs, beaten	2 large eggs, beaten
a little additional orange juice	a little additional orange juice

Soak the dried fruit overnight in the orange juice.

Preheat the oven to gas mark 4 (180°C/350°F).

Place the flour in a bowl and rub in the butter until the mixture resembles breadcrumbs. Stir in the soaked dried fruit and their juice. Add the beaten eggs and sufficient additional orange juice to give the consistency of thick cream. Spoon into an oiled 17.5cm (7 ins) cake tin and bake for 55–60 minutes.

Leave to cool in the tin for 10 minutes before turning out onto a wire cooling rack.

Date and Walnut Cake

Metric/Imperial	American
175 g/6 oz dried dates, pitted and chopped	1½ cups dried dates, pitted and chopped
175 ml/6 fl oz milk	¾ cup milk
50 g/2 oz butter, softened	¼ cup butter, softened
2 large eggs	2 large eggs
60 ml/4 tbsps soya oil	4 tbsps soy oil
175 g/6 oz wholewheat SR flour	1¼ cups wholewheat flour sifted with baking powder
5 ml/1 tsp ground mixed spice	1tsp ground mixed spice
50 g/2 oz porridge oats	1 cup rolled oats
50 g/2 oz walnuts, chopped	½ cup walnuts, chopped

Preheat the oven to gas mark 4 (180°C/350°F).

Put the chopped dates and the milk in a pan and bring to the boil. Leave aside to cool. Drain the dates and reserve the liquid. Blend half the dates, the butter, oil, eggs and date milk together until smooth and creamy. Mix the flour and mixed spice together in a bowl and gradually add the blended ingredients. Fold in the remaining dates and the walnuts and spoon into an oiled and lined 900 g/2 lb loaf tin and cook for one hour.

Guinness Cake

One of my favourite cakes. It is a rich fruit cake full of crunchy walnuts and distinctly flavoured with Guinness. It is best left for 6–8 weeks to mature before being eaten although I must admit that temptation sometimes gets the better of me!

Metric/Imperial	American
225 g/8 oz dried dates, pitted and chopped	2 cups dried dates, pitted and chopped
150–175 ml/5–6 fl oz Guinness	½ cup Guinness
175 g/6 oz butter, softened	¾ cup butter, softened
4 medium eggs	4 medium eggs
275 g/10 oz wholewheat flour	2 cups wholewheat flour
10 ml/2 tsps ground mixed spice	2 tsps ground mixed spice
10 ml/2 tsps baking powder	2 tsps baking powder
550 g/1¼ lbs mixed dried fruit	1¼ lbs mixed dried fruit
100 g/4 oz walnuts, chopped	a scant 1 cup walnuts, chopped

Preheat the oven to gas mark 3 (160°C/325°F).

Place the chopped dates and 90 ml/6 tbsps of Guinness in a pan and cook gently for 5–10 minutes until soft. Blend the butter, eggs and cooked dates together until smooth and creamy. Mix the wholewheat flour, mixed spice and baking powder together in a bowl and gradually fold in the blended ingredients. Add the mixed dried fruit and the chopped walnuts. It may be necessary to add a little more Guinness if the mixture is very stiff. Spoon the mixture into an oiled and lined 17.5cm (7 ins) cake tin, making a shallow dip in the centre. Bake for 1 hour and then reduce the oven temperature to gas mark 2 (150°C/300°F) and cook for a further 1¼ hours. Leave the cake to cool in the tin for 15 minutes before turning out onto a wire rack.

When the cake is cold turn it upside down and prick the base with a thin skewer. Gradually spoon over the remaining Guinness and when it has all been absorbed wrap the cake in greaseproof paper and tin foil and leave to mature.

Date Loaf

Metric/Imperial
225 g/8 oz dried dates, pitted and chopped
175 ml/6 fl oz water
2.5 ml/½ tsp ground cinnamon
225 g/8 oz wholewheat flour
25 g/1 oz soya flour
5 ml/1 tsp baking powder
150 g/5 oz butter
1 large egg, beaten
60 ml/4 tbsps milk

American
2 cups dried dates, pitted and chopped
¾ cup water
½ tsp ground cinnamon
1½ cups wholewheat flour
¼ cup soy flour
1 tsp baking powder
a scant ¾ cup butter
1 large egg, beaten
4 tbsps milk

Preheat the oven to gas mark 4 (180°C/350°F).

Cook the dates gently in the water for 10 minutes until soft. Stir in the ground cinnamon and leave aside to cool. Mix the wholewheat flour, soya flour and baking powder together in a bowl. Rub the butter into the flours until the mixture resembles breadcrumbs. Add the dates, cooking liquid, egg and milk. Spoon the mixture into an oiled and lined 900 g/2 lb loaf tin and bake for 45–50 minutes.

Rich Fruit Cake

A moist, dark fruit cake, ideal for all family parties and celebrations.

Metric/Imperial
175 g/6 oz dried dates, pitted and chopped
150 ml/5 fl oz water
150 g/ 5 oz butter
3 medium eggs
225 g/8 oz wholewheat flour
10 ml/2 tsps baking powder
5 ml/1 tsp ground mixed spice
25 g/1 oz ground almonds
450 g/1 lb mixed dried fruit

to glaze
15 ml/1 tbsp sugarless apricot jam

American
1½ cups dried dates, pitted and chopped
½ cup water
a scant ¾ cup butter
3 medium eggs
1½ cups wholewheat flour
2 tsps baking powder
1 tsp ground mixed spice
¼ cup ground almonds
1 lb mixed dried fruit

to glaze
1 tbsp sugarless apricot jam

Preheat the oven to gas mark 3 (160°C/325°F).

Gently cook the dates in the water for 10 minutes until soft. Leave to cool. Blend the butter, eggs, cooked dates and cooking liquid together until smooth and creamy. Mix the wholewheat flour, baking powder and mixed spice together in a bowl. Fold in the blended ingredients. Add the ground almonds and mixed dried fruit. Spoon into an oiled and lined 17.5cm (7 ins) cake tin, making a small hollow in the centre of the mixture. Bake for 1 hour. Reduce the oven temperature to gas mark 2 (150°C/300°F) and cook for a further hour.

Leave to cool in the tin for 15 minutes before placing on a wire cooling rack. Brush with the apricot jam to glaze.

Simnel Cake

A delicious fruit cake baked with a layer of almond paste in the middle and topped with small almond paste balls. It is traditional in Britain to eat simnel cake at Easter and the eleven marzipan balls used to decorate the cake are said to represent the worthy apostles.

Metric/Imperial
almond paste
225 g/8 oz ground almonds
30 ml/2 tbsps clear honey
a little natural un-sweetened apple juice

cake

150 ml/5 fl oz water
175 g/6 oz dried dates, pitted and chopped
175 g/6 oz butter, softened
3 large eggs
250 g/9 oz wholewheat SR flour
2.5 ml/½ tsp ground mixed spice
2.5 ml/½ tsp almond essence
550 g/1¼ lbs mixed dried fruit
100 g/4 oz mixed peel

to glaze
a little beaten egg

American
almond paste
2 cups ground almonds
2 tbsps clear honey
a little natural un-sweetened apple juice

cake

½ cup water
1½ cups dried dates, pitted and chopped
¾ cup butter, softened
3 large eggs
1¾ cups wholewheat flour sifted with baking powder
½ tsp ground mixed spice
½ tsp almond extract
1¼ lbs mixed dried fruit
¾ cup mixed peel

to glaze
a little beaten egg

Preheat the oven to gas mark 3 (160°C/325°F).

First prepare the almond paste. Mix the ground almonds together with the honey and sufficient fruit juice to form a fairly stiff paste. Divide the paste in two and roll out one piece on a lightly floured board to the shape and size of the base of the cake tin to be used. Make a narrow ring with some of the remaining almond paste, to fit round the top of the finished cake. Divide the rest of the paste into eleven pieces and shape into small balls. Set aside until needed.

Cook the dates in the water for 10 minutes until soft. Leave to cool. Blend the dates, cooking liquid, butter and eggs together until smooth and creamy. Mix the wholewheat SR flour and mixed spice together in a bowl and gradually fold in the blended ingredients. Add the almond essence, mixed dried fruit and mixed peel. Place half the cake mixture in an oiled and lined 17.5cm (7 ins) cake tin and lay the round of almond paste on top. Spoon over the remaining cake mixture and make a small hollow in the top of the cake. Bake for 1 hour, then reduce the temperature to gas mark 1 (140°C/275°F) and cook for a further 1¼–1½ hours. Leave the cake in the tin for 15 minutes before turning out onto a wire cooling rack.

Brush the remaining pieces of almond paste with the beaten egg and place the ring around the top of the cake. Arrange the balls on top of the ring and press down lightly. Put the cake back in the oven preheated to gas mark 4 (180°C/350°F) for 10–15 minutes until the almond paste is golden brown.

Malt Loaf

A moist, rich, yeasted tea bread.

Metric/Imperial	American
450 g/1lb wholewheat flour	1 lb wholewheat flour
25 g/1 oz fresh yeast or 7 ml/1½ tsps dried yeast	/1½ tsps active dry yeast
275 ml/10 fl oz tepid water	1¼ cups tepid water
225 g/8 oz unbleached white flour	1½ cups unbleached white flour
350 g/12 oz sultanas	2¼ cups white seedless raisins
45 ml/3 tbsps soya oil	3 tbsps soy oil
45 ml/3 tbsps malt extract	3 tbsps malt extract
15 ml/1 tbsp molasses	1 tbsp molasses
250 ml/9 fl oz tepid water	1 cup tepid water

Place 100 g/4 oz (1 cup) of wholewheat flour in a small bowl. Cream the yeast with 275 ml/10 fl oz (1¼ cups) tepid water before mixing with the flour. Leave in a warm place for 15–20 minutes until frothy.

Put the remaining flour, the sultanas and soya oil in a large bowl and mix together. Stir the malt extract and molasses into the remaining tepid water until well blended. Pour the wet ingredients and the yeast mixture into the dry ingredients and mix to form a slightly sticky dough. Cover and leave in a warm place to double in size.

Turn onto a floured board and knead lightly until smooth and elastic. Cut into shape and place the dough in one oiled 900 g (2 lb) and one oiled 450 g (1 lb) loaf tin. Cover and leave in a warm place to prove.

Preheat the oven to gas mark 5 (190°C/375°F) and bake for 50–55 minutes, covering the crusts with aluminium foil if they seem likely to become too dark. Tip the malt loaves out onto a rack to cool. Tap the bottom of each loaf and if it sounds hollow it is a good sign that the bread is done.

Guernsey Gâche

A spiced, fruit loaf traditionally made in Guernsey. This recipe is adapted from the one still used by my father-in-law, a Guernsey man. The fermentation of the yeast is retarded slightly by the inclusion of dried fruit and mixed peel and additional time must be allowed for rising and proving the bread.

Metric/Imperial	American
675 g/1½ lbs wholewheat flour	1½ lbs wholewheat flour
25 g/1 oz fresh yeast or 7g/1½ tsps dried yeast	1½ tsps active dry yeast
275 ml/10 fl oz tepid water	1¼ cups tepid water
50 g/2 oz butter	¼ cup butter
45 ml/3 tbsps corn oil	3 tbsps corn oil
175 g/6 oz sultanas	1 cup white seedless raisins
175 g/6 oz raisins	1 cup raisins
100 g/4 oz mixed peel	¾ cup mixed peel
1 whole nutmeg, grated	1 whole nutmeg, grated
275 ml/10 fl oz tepid milk	1¼ cups tepid milk

Place 100g/4 oz (1 cup) flour in a small bowl. Blend the yeast with 275 ml/10 fl oz (1¼ cups tepid water and mix with the flour. Leave in a warm place for 15–20 minutes until frothy.

Rub the butter into the remaining flour until the mixture resembles fine breadcrumbs. Add the other ingredients and the yeast mixture. Knead together lightly to form a soft dough. Cover and leave in a warm place to double in size.

Knead and cut into shape. Place in two well oiled 900 g/2 lb loaf tins, cover and leave to prove.

Preheat the oven to gas mark 6 (200°C/400°F) and bake for 40–45 minutes. When the loaf is ready it should fall out of the tin easily and will sound hollow when tapped on the bottom.

Easter Tea Ring

Metric/Imperial	American
dough	*dough*
50 g/2 oz butter	¼ cup butter
125 ml/4 fl oz milk	a scant ½ cup milk
15 g/½ oz fresh yeast or	1 tsp active dry yeast
5 ml/1 tsp dried yeast	1 medium egg, beaten
1 medium egg, beaten	1½ cups wholewheat
225 g/8 oz wholewheat	flour
flour	
	filling
filling	2 tbsps butter
25 g/1 oz butter	¼ cup ground almonds
25 g/1 oz ground	½ cup raisins
almonds	½ cup mixed peel
75 g/3 oz raisins	1 tsp ground cinnamon
50 g/2 oz mixed peel	2 eating apples, cored
5 ml/1 tsp ground	and grated
cinnamon	1 medium carrot, finely
2 eating apples, cored	grated
and grated	a few drops of almond
1 medium carrot, finely	extract
grated	
a few drops of almond	*to glaze*
essence	1 egg, beaten
	1 tbsp flaked almonds
to glaze	
1 egg, beaten	
15 g/½ oz flaked	
almonds	

To make the dough, heat the butter and milk together in a pan until the butter has melted. Dissolve the yeast in the tepid mixture. Place the flour in a mixing bowl and stir in the beaten egg and yeasted mixture. Knead to form a dough. Cover and leave in a warm place to double in size. Knead the dough a second time and again leave in a warm place to rise.

To make the filling, melt the butter in a pan. Add all the remaining filling ingredients and mix together well.

Roll out the dough on a lightly floured board until it forms a rectangle 25cm × 15cm (10 ins × 6 ins). The dough should be approximately 0.75cm (¼ in) thick. Spread with the filling mixture. Roll up the dough,

beginning with the wide side. Moisten the edges and pinch together to seal. Twist the dough round into a ring and join the ends together. Cut the ring at 2.5cm (1 in) intervals through three-quarters of the ring.

Brush with a little beaten egg and sprinkle with flaked almonds. Stand in a warm place to prove for 20 minutes. Bake in a preheated oven gas mark 7 (220°C/425°F) for 20–25 minutes.

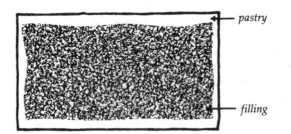

pastry

filling

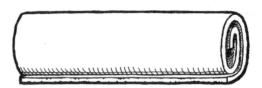

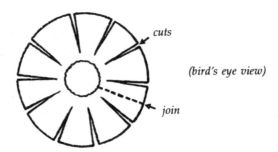

cuts

(bird's eye view)

join

Hot Cross Buns

Metric/Imperial
450 g/1 lb wholewheat
flour
25 g/1 oz fresh yeast or 7
ml/1½ tsps dried yeast
150 ml/5 fl oz tepid milk
150 ml/5 fl oz tepid
water
5 ml/1 tsp ground mixed
spice
2.5 ml/½ tsp ground
cinnamon
2.5 ml/½ tsp ground
nutmeg
50 g/2 oz butter, melted
75 g/3 oz sultanas
75 g/3 oz currants
50 g/2 oz mixed peel
1 medium egg, beaten
5–10 ml/1–2 tsps orange
zest

to decorate
50 g/2 oz short crust
pastry
30 ml/2 tbsps milk
5 ml/1 tsp soya oil

American
1 lb wholewheat flour
1½ tsps active dry yeast
½ cup tepid milk
½ cup tepid water
1 tsp ground mixed spice
½ tsp ground cinnamon
½ tsp ground nutmeg
¼ cup butter, melted
½ cup white seedless
raisins
½ cup currants
½ cup mixed peel
1 medium egg, beaten
1–2 tsps grated orange
rind

to decorate
½ cup short crust pastry
2 tbsps milk
1 tsp soy oil

Another Easter speciality is the hot cross bun, a spiced currant bun decorated with a pastry cross. It is said that food cooked on Good Friday is blessed and hot cross buns baked on that day will not become mouldy. They are reputed to have curative properties and the buns were, in bygone days, kept from one year to the next for medicinal purposes. The smell of hot cross buns cooking in the oven is so tempting that I never have any left to put to the test!

This quantity makes twelve hot cross buns.

Place 100g/4 oz (1 cup) flour in a bowl. Blend the yeast with the tepid milk and water and add to the flour. Leave in a warm place for 15–20 minutes until frothy.

Add the remaining ingredients and mix to form a soft dough. Turn onto a floured board and knead for several minutes, being careful not to add too much flour to the soft dough. Place in a bowl, cover and leave in a warm place to double in size.

Knead again until the dough is smooth and elastic and divide into twelve pieces. Form into small balls and place, well apart, on an oiled baking sheet. Flatten the balls slightly with the fingertips. Cover and leave in a warm place to prove for 30 minutes.

Roll out the short crust pastry and cut into strips 0.75cm (¼ in) wide. Dampen the pastry with a little water and lay two strips across each bun to form a cross. Bake in a preheated oven gas mark 6 (200°C/400°F) for 15–20 minutes.

Place on a wire cooling rack and brush over twice with a mixture of milk and oil. Leave to cool.

Wholewheat Croissants

Croissants are thought to have been made first in Budapest at the end of the fifteenth century. It is said that the bakers of that city, working early in the morning, were able to raise the alarm and prevent a Turkish attack. To celebrate the occasion the bakers fashioned a pastry in the shape of the Turkish symbol, a crescent. Croissants are, however, now associated with France where they are eaten for breakfast. They may be served with butter, apricot jam and cream but I prefer to eat them in a more authentic manner, dunking them in a cup of hot milky coffee.

This quantity makes eight croissants.

Metric/Imperial
100 g/4 oz wholewheat flour
15 g/½ oz fresh yeast or 5 ml/1 tsp dried yeast
50 ml/2 fl oz tepid water
75 ml/3 fl oz tepid milk
5 ml/1 tsp salt
100 g/4 oz unbleached white flour
15 ml/1 tbsp soya oil
100 g/4oz butter

to glaze
1 egg, beaten

American
¾ cup wholewheat flour
1½ tsp active dry yeast
3½ tbsps tepid water
5 tbsps tepid milk
1 tsp salt
¾ cup unbleached white flour
1 tbsp soy oil
½ cup butter

to glaze
1 egg, beaten

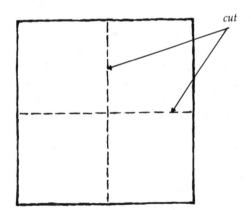

cut

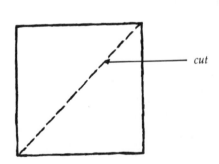

cut

Place the wholewheat flour in a mixing bowl. Blend the yeast with the tepid water and milk and stir into the flour. Leave in a warm place for 15–20 minutes until frothy.

Add the unbleached white flour, the salt and oil and mix together to form a soft dough. Knead until the dough is smooth and elastic. Cover and leave to rise in a warm place until it has doubled in size. Chill for one hour.

Roll out on a floured board to form a rectangle 0.75cm (¼ in) thick. Soften the butter with a knife and divide into three pieces. Using the first portion of butter cover two thirds of the dough with evenly spaced dabs of fat. Fold the ends of the dough into the centre, making sure that the unbuttered section is in the middle. Seal the edges and turn the dough through 90°. Repeat the rolling, buttering and folding twice more. Wrap the dough in greaseproof paper and chill for two hours.

Roll out to form a square measuring 35cm (14 ins), working as quickly as possible and in a cool place. Trim the edges of the dough and cut into four squares. Cut each piece in half diagonally to make two triangles. Roll up each triangle loosely, starting with the wide edge and finishing with the tip underneath. Place on a lightly floured baking tray and gently bend into crescent shapes. Cover and prove in a warm place until well risen and springy.

Brush with a little beaten egg and bake in a preheated oven gas mark 7 (220°C/425°F) for 5 minutes. Reduce the oven temperature to gas mark 5 (190°C/375°F) and bake for a further 10–15 minutes until golden brown.

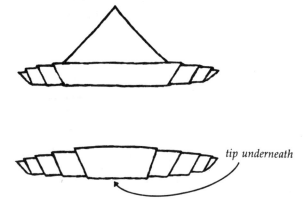

tip underneath

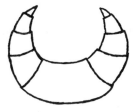

Puddings

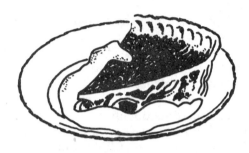

Peach and Orange Quiche

A light, creamy, fresh fruit tart that can be eaten warm or cold.

Metric/Imperial

pastry
175 g/6 oz wholewheat flour
50 g/2 oz soya flour
75 g/3 oz butter
45 ml/3 tbsps soya oil
35–40 ml/7–8 tsps cold water

filling
2 ripe peaches
225 g/8 oz natural cottage cheese
150 ml/5 fl oz natural unsweetened orange juice
2 large eggs
5 ml/1 tsp orange zest (optional)

American

pastry
1¼ cups wholewheat flour
½ cup soy flour
a scant ½ cup butter
3 tbsp soy oil
7–8 tsps cold water

filling
2 ripe peaches
1 cup unflavoured cottage cheese
½ cup natural un-sweetened orange juice
2 large eggs
1 tsp grated orange rind (optional)

Preheat the oven to gas mark 5 (190°C/375°F).

To make the pastry, mix the wholewheat flour and soya flour together in a bowl. Rub in the butter and oil until the mixture resembles breadcrumbs. Add the water and press together to form a dough. Roll out on a floured board and line a 20cm (8 ins) oiled flan ring.

Slice the peaches and arrange on top of the pastry. Blend the cottage cheese, orange juice and eggs together until smooth and creamy. Pour the mixture over the peaches and sprinkle with the orange zest. Bake for 25 minutes until firm to the touch.

Leave to cool.

Yorkshire Curd Tart

A delicious soft cheese tart, sweetened and flavoured with currants and apple juice. Sieved cottage cheese can be used if fresh curd is unobtainable.

Metric/Imperial	American
pastry	*pastry*
225 g/8 oz wholewheat flour	1½ cups wholewheat flour
100 g/ 4 oz butter	½ cup butter
40 ml/8 tsps cold water	8 tsps cold water
filling	*filling*
50 g/2 oz butter	¼ cup butter
100 g/4 oz currants	¾ cup currants
15–30 ml/1–2 tbsps concentrated apple juice	1–2 tbsps concentrated apple juice
225 g/8 oz curd	1 cup curd
2 large eggs, beaten	2 large eggs, beaten

Preheat the oven to gas mark 6 (200°C/400°F).

To make the pastry, place the flour in a bowl and rub in the butter until the mixture resembles breadcrumbs. Add the water and press together lightly with the fingertips to form a dough. Roll out on a floured board and line a 20cm (8 ins) oiled flan ring.

To make the filling, put the butter, currants and apple concentrate in a pan and heat gently until the butter has melted. Remove from the heat and stir in the curd and beaten eggs. Pour the filling mixture into the pastry case and bake for 25 minutes until golden brown and firm to the touch.

Serve warm or cold.

Lemon Pudding

A fresh, tangy lemon sauce topped with a light sponge.

Metric/Imperial	American
225 ml/8 fl oz milk	1 cup milk
30 ml/2 tbsps honey	2 tbsps honey
2 large eggs	2 large eggs
25 g/1 oz wholewheat SR flour	1 tbsp wholewheat flour sifted with baking powder
15 g/½ oz butter	1 tbsp butter
juice and grated rind of 1 lemon	juice and grated rind of 1 lemon

Preheat the oven to gas mark 4 (180°C/350°F).

Heat the milk and honey together gently until well mixed. Leave aside to cool. Separate the eggs and stir the yolks into the tepid milk and honey mixture.

Place the flour in a small bowl and rub in the butter until the mixture resembles breadcrumbs. Stir in the egg mixture, lemon zest and lemon juice. Stiffly beat the egg whites and fold into the mixture. Pour into an oiled pie dish and stand in a deep baking tray, filled with warm water. Bake for 40–45 minutes until firm to the touch.

Pear and Apple Charlotte

A traditional family pudding.

Metric/Imperial	American
6–7 slices of wholewheat bread	6–7 slices wholewheat bread
75–90 ml/5–6 tbsps melted butter	5–6 tbsps melted butter
2 large pears	2 large pears
2 large Cox's eating apples	2 large Cox's eating apples
25 g/1 oz butter	2 tbsps butter
50 g/2 oz sultanas	¼ cup white seedless raisins
3–4 drops of vanilla essence	3–4 drops of vanilla extract

Preheat the oven to gas mark 6 (200°C/400°F).

Remove the crusts from the bread and brush both sides of each slice with melted butter. Line a well oiled 1 litre (1¾ pint) pudding basin with most of the bread, making sure that there are no gaps in the lining.

Wash, core and slice the apples and pears and cook them gently in the 25g/1 oz (2 tbsps) butter until soft. Beat in the vanilla essence and add the sultanas. Spoon the fruit purée into the basin and place a layer of buttered bread on the top. Cover with a well fitting lid or plate and stand a 1 kilo (2 lb) weight on the top. Bake for 30 minutes.

Remove the weight and the plate and cook for a further 10 minutes.

Tip upside down onto a serving dish.

Orange and Apricot Soufflé

Metric/ Imperial	American
175 g/6 oz dried apricots, chopped	1½ cups dried apricots, chopped
275 ml/10 fl oz natural unsweetened orange juice	1¼ cups natural unsweetened orange juice
10 ml/2 tsps orange zest	2 tsps grated orange rind
75g/3 oz ground almonds	¾ cups ground almonds
4 egg whites	4 egg whites

Preheat the oven to gas mark 6 (200°C/400°F).

Put the apricots in a pan with the orange juice and bring to the boil. Simmer for 10 minutes. Leave aside to cool. Blend until smooth. Stir in the orange zest and ground almonds. Beat the egg whites until stiff and peaked. Fold into the mixture and spoon into a soufflé dish. Bake for 25 minutes until golden brown and firm to touch.

French Apple Tart

A classic dish that is traditionally rich in butter and sugar. The sweetness in this recipe is provided naturally by the use of eating apples and fruit juice. The tart is also brushed with sugarless apricot jam to give it an attractive glaze.

Metric/Imperial

pastry
225 g/8 oz wholewheat flour
100 g/4 oz butter
1 egg
30 ml/6 tsps cold water
3–4 drops of almond essence

filling
900 g/2 lbs eating apples
60 ml/4 tbsps natural unsweetened apple juice
grated rind of 1 lemon
10 ml/2 tsps arrowroot
15 ml/1 tbsp cold water

to glaze
1 red eating apple
30 ml/2 tbsps sugarless apricot jam

American

pastry
1½ cups wholewheat flour
½ cup butter
1 egg
6 tsps cold water
3–4 drops of almond extract

filling
2 lbs eating apples
4 tbsps natural un-sweetened apple juice
grated rind of 1 lemon
2 tsps arrowroot
1 tbsp cold water

to glaze
1 red eating apple
2 tbsps sugarless apricot jam

Preheat the oven to gas mark 6 (200°C/400°F).

To make the pastry put the flour in a bowl and rub in the butter until the mixture resembles breadcrumbs. Separate the egg and stir the egg yolk and almond essence into the bowl. Gradually add the water and press together lightly with the fingertips to form a pastry dough. Roll out on a floured board and line a 20cm (8 ins) flan ring. Prick the pastry base with a fork and blind bake for 8 minutes. Brush with the egg white and bake for a further 5 minutes.

Core, peel and slice the apples. Cook gently in the apple juice until soft. Beat with a fork to form a purée. Dissolve the arrowroot in 15 ml/1 tbsp cold water. Stir in the apple purée and bring to the boil. Cook gently for 1–2 minutes, stirring all the time. Leave to cool slightly before spooning into the pastry case.

Core and slice the red apple and arrange on the top of the tart. Brush with half of the apricot jam and bake for 20 minutes. Remove from the oven and brush with the remaining jam. Leave to cool.

apple slices overlapping in concentric circles

flan ring

Milk Pudding

Metric/Imperial
50 g/2 oz creamed coconut
575 ml/1 pint skimmed milk
75 g/3 oz sultanas
25 g/1 oz brown rice flour

American
¼ cup creamed coconut
2½ cups skimmed milk
½ cup white seedless raisins
1 tbsp brown rice flour

Preheat the oven to gas mark 3 (170°C/325°F).

Put the creamed coconut in a pan with the milk and heat gently until melted. Blend together with three quarters of the sultanas. Return to the pan and bring to the boil. Gradually stir in the rice flour and the remaining sultanas. Simmer gently for 5–10 minutes until the mixture thickens. Pour into an ovenproof dish and bake for 30 minutes until lightly browned.

Pears Baked with Fig Syrup

Metric/Imperial	American
100 g/4 oz dried figs, chopped	1 cup dried figs, chopped
2.5 ml/½ tsp ground ginger	½ tsp ground ginger
150 ml/5 fl oz natural unsweetened apple juice	½ cup natural unsweetened apple juice
4 ripe dessert pears	4 ripe dessert pears

Preheat the oven to gas mark 3 (170°C/325°F).

Put the figs, ground ginger and apple juice in a pan and bring to the boil. Simmer for 5 minutes. Drain and reserve the juice.

Cut the base from each pear and remove the core with a sharp knife or spoon. Fill the hollow with figs and stand in an overnproof dish. Pour over the juice and bake for 20–30 minutes until the pears are tender.

Pears with Cheese

If Wensleydale cheese is unavailable use another sharp, crumbly white cheese.

Metric/Imperial	American
4 ripe pears	4 ripe pears
225 g/8 oz Wensleydale cheese	½ lb white cheese

Preheat the oven to gas mark 7 (210°C/425°F).

Wash the pears and remove the cores. Slice each pear into 4 individual ovenproof dishes. Grate the cheese over the top of the fruit. Bake for 10 minutes until the cheese has melted and is golden brown on top.

Gooseberry Tart

Agar agar has similar culinary uses to gelatine. I use it with natural fruit juices to make glazes and jellies. It has, however, different melting and setting points to gelatine — it dissolves in boiling water and sets when lukewarm (40°–44°C/104°–111°F).

Metric/Imperial	American
pastry	*pastry*
75 g/3 oz wholewheat SR flour	½ cup wholewheat flour sifted with baking powder
75 g/3 oz butter	a scant ½ cup butter
75 g/3 oz ground almonds	¾ cup ground almonds
1 egg yolk	1 egg yolk
3–4 drops of almond essence	3–4 drops almond extract
20–30 ml/4–6 tsps cold water	4–6 tsps cold water
filling	*filling*
450 g/1 lb ripe gooseberries	1 lb ripe gooseberries
275–350 ml/10–12 fl oz natural unsweetened apple juice	1¼–1½ cups natural unsweetened apple juice
5 ml/1 tsp agar agar	1 tsp agar agar

Preheat the oven to gas mark 7 (220°C/425°F).

To make the pastry, place the flour in a bowl and rub in the butter. Add the ground almonds, egg yolk and almond essence. Mix together well. Add sufficient water to form a pastry dough. Roll out on a floured board and line an oiled 20cm (8 ins) flan ring. Prick the pastry base with a fork several times. Line the pastry with crumpled greaseproof paper and fill with dried beans. Bake for 15 minutes. Remove the beans and greaseproof paper and cook the pastry for a further 10–15 minutes. Leave to cool before removing the flan ring.

Top and tail the gooseberries and cook gently in the apple juice until tender. Drain and reserve the juice. Arrange the gooseberries in the bottom of the pastry case. Make the cooking juice up to 275 ml/10 fl oz (1¼ cups) with apple juice. Dissolve the agar agar in 60 ml/ 4 tbsps (4 tbsps) cold juice. Add the remaining juice and bring it to the boil, stirring frequently. Boil gently for 2–3 minutes until it begins to thicken. Cool slightly before pouring over the gooseberries.

Leave to set.

Apricot Crumble

Metric/Imperial	American
filling	*filling*
225 g/8 oz dried apricots	2 cups dried apricots
575 ml/1 pt water	2½ cups water
topping	*topping*
50 g/2 oz wholewheat flour	2 tbsps wholewheat flour
75 g/3 oz porridge oats	1½ cups rolled oats
15 g/½ oz desiccated coconut	¼ cup dried coconut
90 ml/6 tbsps soya oil	6 tbsps soy oil

Preheat the oven to gas mark 5 (190°C/375°F).

Soak the dried apricots in water overnight. Place in a pan with 575 ml/1 pint (2½ cups) water and simmer gently for 10 minutes until soft. Drain and reserve the juice. Put the apricots in a pie dish and pour over sufficient juice to cover the bottom of the dish.

To make the topping, mix the wholewheat flour, porridge oats and coconut together in a bowl. Rub in the oil and sprinkle over the cooked apricots. Bake for 25–30 minutes.

Serve with a fruit sauce made by thickening the remaining apricot juice with a little arrowroot.

ARROWROOT can be used to thicken any fruit juice or fruit purée. I suggest using 5 ml/1 heaped tsp (1 tsp) to every 150 ml/5 fl oz (½ cup) of purée or liquid. Blend the arrowroot with 10 ml/2 tsps (2 tsps) of cold water before adding to the other ingredients. Heat slowly, stirring all the time until the sauce thickens.

Baked Egg Custard

A dish popular with the entire family.

Metric/Imperial	American
pastry	*pastry*
225 g/8 oz wholewheat flour	1½ cups wholewheat flour
75 g/3 oz butter	a scant ½ cup butter
45 ml/3 tbsps corn oil	3 tbsps corn oil
35–40 ml/7–8 tsps cold water	7–8 tsps cold water
filling	*filling*
425 ml/15 fl oz milk	1¾ cups milk
25 ml/1½ tbsps honey	1½ tbsps honey
3 medium eggs	3 medium eggs
1 egg yolk	1 egg yolk
3–4 drops of vanilla essence	3–4 drops of vanilla extract
a little freshly grated nutmeg	a little freshly grated nutmeg

Preheat the oven to gas mark 6 (200°C/400°F).

Place the flour in a bowl and rub in the butter and oil until the mixture resembles breadcrumbs. Add the water and press together lightly with the fingertips to form a pastry dough. Roll out on a floured board and line an oiled 20cm (8 ins) pie dish. Lightly prick the pastry base with a fork.

To make the filling, heat the milk and honey together gently in a pan until blended. Whisk the eggs, egg yolk and vanilla essence together and pour into the pan with the other ingredients. Mix gently, being careful not to beat. Place the pie dish on a baking tray and pour the custard into the pastry case. Sprinkle the nutmeg over the top and bake for 10 minutes. Reduce the oven temperature to gas mark 4 (180°C/350°F) and cook for a further 20 minutes until set. To test the custard push the sharp point of a knife into the centre, when the blade comes out clean and custard is cooked.

Leave to cool before serving.

Apricot Frangipane

A delicious tart that can be served hot or cold. The pastry base is covered with apricot purée and an almond and orange flavoured topping.

Metric/Imperial	American
filling	*filling*
100 g/4 oz dried apricots	1 cup dried apricots
275 ml/10 fl oz water	1¼ cups water
pastry	*pastry*
225 g/8 oz wholewheat flour	1½ cups wholewheat flour
125 g/4½ oz butter	½ cup butter
35–40 ml/7–8 tsps cold water	7–8 tsps cold water
3–4 drops of almond essence	3–4 drops of almond extract
topping	*topping*
50 g/2 oz butter	¼ cup butter
1 medium egg	1 medium egg
50 g/2 oz ground almonds	½ cup ground almonds
25 g/1 oz wholewheat SR flour	1 tbsp wholewheat flour sifted with baking powder
30–45 ml/2–3 tbsps fresh orange juice	2–3 tbsps fresh orange juice
15 g/½ oz flaked almonds	1 tbsp flaked almonds

Preheat the oven to gas mark 5 (190°C/375°F).

Soak the apricots overnight in water. Place them in a pan with 275 ml/10 fl oz (1¼ cups) water and cook gently until soft. Purée and leave aside to cool.

To make the pastry, put the wholewheat flour in a bowl and rub in the butter until the mixture resembles breadcrumbs. Add the water and almond essence and press together with the fingertips to form a dough. Roll out on a floured board and line an oiled 20cm (8 ins) flan ring. Prick the pastry base with a fork.

To make the topping, soften the remaining butter and blend together with the egg until light and creamy. Fold in the wholewheat SR flour and the ground almonds. Add sufficient orange juice to form a soft dropping consistency. Spread the apricot purée over the pastry base, pour the almond mixture on the top and sprinkle with the flaked almonds. Bake for 25 minutes until firm to the touch.

Gooseberry and Elderflower Pie

Surely it must be more than sheer coincidence that gooseberries are available while the elderflower is in full bloom. The two complement each other perfectly, creating a sweet, fragrant flavour reminiscent of muscatel grapes.

Metric/Imperial	American
filling	*filling*
450 g/1 lb ripe gooseberries	1 lb ripe gooseberries
90 ml/6 tbsps natural unsweetened apple juice	6 tbsps natural unsweetened apple juice
5–7 sprigs of elderflowers, stalks removed	5–7 sprigs of elderflowers, stalks removed
pastry	*pastry*
150 g/5 oz wholewheat flour	1 cup wholewheat flour
25 g/1 oz soya flour	¼ cup soy flour
50 g/2 oz butter	¼ cup butter
30 ml/2 tbsps soya oil	2 tbsps soy oil
30 ml/2 tbsps cold water	2 tbsps cold water
to glaze	*to glaze*
a little beaten egg	a little beaten egg

Preheat the oven to gas mark 6 (200°C/400°F).

Top and tail the gooseberries and place them in the bottom of a pie dish with the apple juice and the elderflowers.

To make the pastry, mix the wholewheat flour and soya flour together in a bowl. Rub in the butter and the oil until the mixture resembles breadcrumbs. Gradually add the water and press together lightly with the fingertips to form a dough. Roll out on a floured board and cut out a circle 1.25 cm (½ in) larger than the top of the pie dish. Carefully trim 1.25 cm (½ in) from the pastry circle and lay the strip around the dampened edge of the pie dish. Moisten the edge of the pastry circle and lay it over the fruit. Press the pastry edges together to seal, and brush the top with a little beaten egg. Bake for 25 minutes.

Cherry Tart

A fresh fruit tart served with natural yoghurt or cream is one of the most popular puddings. This recipe uses cherries but any fresh, ripe fruit can be used with the same degree of success.

Metric/Imperial	American
pastry	*pastry*
150 g/5 oz wholewheat flour	1 cup wholewheat flour
25 g/1 oz maize meal	1 tbsp corn meal
90 g/3½ oz butter	½ cup butter
25–30 ml/5–6 tsps cold water	5–6 tsps cold water
filling	*filling*
450 g/1 lb ripe cherries	1 lb ripe cherries
275 ml/10 fl oz natural unsweetened red grape juice	1¼ cups natural unsweetened red grape juice
10 ml/2 tsps arrowroot	2 tsps arrowroot

Preheat the oven to gas mark 6 (200°C/400°F).

Mix the wholewheat flour and maize meal together in a bowl. Rub in the butter until the mixture resembles breadcrumbs. Gradually add the water and press together with the fingertips to form a pastry dough. Roll out on a floured board and line a 15–17cm (6–7 ins) flan ring. Prick the pastry base lightly with a fork and line with crumpled greaseproof paper. Fill with dried beans and bake for 15 minutes. Remove the beans and greaseproof paper and return to the oven for 10–15 minutes. Leave to cool.

Wash and stone the cherries and arrange on the cooked pastry case. Blend the arrowroot in 30–45 ml/2–3 tbsps (2–3 tbsps) of grape juice. Add the remaining juice and bring to the boil. Simmer gently until it begins to thicken and becomes clear. Cool slightly before pouring over the fruit.

Chill until set. Serve cold.

New England Plum Pie

An unusual pie filling with an American flavour, the richness of sweet plump prunes being the perfect foil for slightly sharper dessert plums.

Metric/Imperial	American
filling	*filling*
225 g/8 oz dessert plums	½ lb dessert plums
100 g/4 oz prunes	1 cup prunes
15 g/½ oz butter	1 tbsp butter
pastry	*pastry*
225 g/8 oz wholewheat flour	1½ cups wholewheat flour
150 g/5 oz butter	½ cup butter
25–30 ml/5–6 tsps cold water	5–6 tsps cold water
1 egg yolk	1 egg yolk
5 ml/1 tsp lemon juice	1 tsp lemon juice
to glaze	*to glaze*
a little milk	a little milk

Preheat the oven to gas mark 6 (200°C/400°F).

Soak the prunes overnight. Barely cover with water and bring to the boil. Simmer gently until plump and tender. Drain and leave to cool.

To make the pastry, place the flour in a bowl and rub in the butter until the mixture resembles breadcrumbs. Add half the egg yolk, the lemon juice and sufficient water to form a pastry dough. Roll out three quarters of the pastry and line a 20cm (8 ins) oiled pie dish. Prick the pastry base with a fork and brush with the remaining egg yolk. Bake for 8–10 minutes.

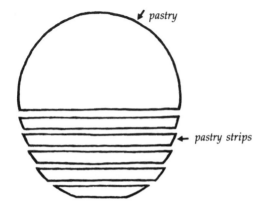

pastry

pastry strips

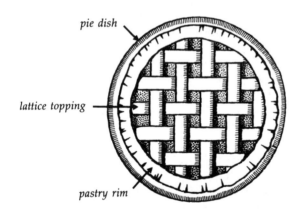

pie dish

lattice topping

pastry rim

Apricot Crème en Croûte

A light, nutty pastry case filled with fresh apricots and a creamy custard.

Metric/Imperial	American
pastry	*pastry*
175 g/6 oz wholewheat flour	1¼ cups wholewheat flour
25 g/1 oz soya flour	¼ cup soy flour
25 g/1 oz maize meal	1 tbsp corn meal
75 g/3 oz butter	a scant ½ cup butter
30 ml/2 tbsps soya oil	2 tbsps soy oil
1 egg yolk	1 egg yolk
30–45 ml/2–3 tbsps cold water	2–3 tbsps cold water
filling	*filling*
100 g/4 oz natural cottage cheese	½ cup unflavoured cottage cheese
275 ml/10 fl oz natural yoghurt	1¼ cups unflavoured yoghurt
45 ml/3 tbsps clear honey	3 tbsps clear honey
1 orange	1 orange
3 egg yolks	3 egg yolks
225 g/8 oz ripe apricots	½ lb ripe apricots
275 ml/10 fl oz water	1¼ cups water
10 ml/2 tsps arrowroot	2 tsps arrowroot

Stone the plums and prunes and arrange on top of the pastry case. Dot with 15g/½ oz (1 tbsp) butter. Roll out the remaining pastry and cut into 1.25cm (½ in) strips. Lay the pastry strips across the pie dish to form a lattice. Moisten the edges with a little water and press onto the rim of the dish. Trim away surplus pastry and brush with milk. Bake for 30–35 minutes.

Preheat the oven to gas mark 6 (200°C/400°F).

Mix the wholewheat flour, soya flour and maize meal together in a bowl. Rub in the butter and oil until the mixture resembles breadcrumbs. Add the egg yolk and sufficient water to form a pastry dough. Roll out on a floured board and line a 20cm (8 ins) oiled flan ring. Lightly prick the pastry base with a fork and line with crumpled greaseproof paper. Fill with dried beans and bake for 15 minutes. Remove the beans and greaseproof paper and cook for a further 10–15 minutes.

To make the filling, press the cottage cheese through a sieve into a small bowl. Add the yoghurt, 30 ml/2 tbsps (2 tbsps) clear honey and the grated rind of the orange. Place the bowl in a pan of warm water and heat gently until the mixture is lukewarm. Stir in the three egg yolks and continue cooking for 10–15 minutes until the mixture begins to thicken. Cool slightly. Pour into the pastry case and chill until set.

Wash and stone the apricots. Place them in a pan with the cut sides uppermost. Dissolve 15 ml/1 tbsp (1 tbsp) clear honey in 275 g/10 fl oz (1¼ cups) of water and pour over the fruit. Poach gently for 5–10 minutes until tender. Remove the apricots with a slotted spoon and leave aside. Blend the arrowroot with the juice of the orange before adding to the remaining honeyed water in the pan. Gradually bring to the boil, stirring continuously until the mixture thickens. Arrange the apricots on top of the custard and cover with the fruit glaze.

Leave to cool.

Banana and Fig Crumble

Metric/Imperial	American
filling	*filling*
3 ripe bananas	3 ripe bananas
100 g/4 oz dried figs	1 cup dried figs
150 ml/5 fl oz water	½ cup water
topping	*topping*
75 g/3 oz wholewheat flour	½ cup wholewheat flour
50 g/2 oz porridge oats	1 cup rolled oats
75 g/3 oz butter	a scant ½ cup butter
25 g/1 oz sesame seeds	¼ cup sesame seeds

Preheat the oven to gas mark 5 (190°C/375°F).

Chop the figs, remove the tough stalks and cook in the water for 10–15 minutes until they begin to soften. Drain and reserve the juice. Slice the bananas and mix with the cooked figs. Place in a pie dish and pour over sufficient juice to cover the bottom of the dish.

Mix the flour and porridge oats together in a bowl and rub in the butter. Add the sesame seeds. Sprinkle the crumble over the fruit, press down lightly and bake for 25–30 minutes.

Date and Apple Pudding

Any dried fruit could be used in this recipe.
Figs and apples make a delicious alternative.

Metric/Imperial	American
filling	*filling*
100 g/4 oz dried dates, pitted and chopped	1 cup dried dates, pitted and chopped
125 ml/4 fl oz water	½ cup water
450/1 lb eating apples, cored	1 lb eating apples, cored
5 ml/1 tsp ground cinnamon	1 tsp ground cinnamon
25 g/1 oz butter	2 tbsps butter
topping	*topping*
2 large eggs	2 large eggs
50 g/2 oz fresh wholewheat breadcrumbs	½ cup fresh wholewheat breadcrumbs
50 g/2 oz desiccated coconut	1 cup dried coconut
75 ml/5 tbsps natural yoghurt	5 tbsps unflavoured yoghurt

Preheat the oven to gas mark 5 (190°C/375°F).

Place the dates in a pan with the water and cook gently for 10 minutes until they begin to soften. Slice the apples and mix with the cooked dates. Spoon into an ovenproof dish and add sufficient cooking liquid or water to cover the bottom of the dish. Sprinkle the cinnamon over the top and dot with butter.

To make the topping, separate the eggs and mix the yolks with the breadcrumbs, coconut and yoghurt. Beat the egg whites until stiff and fold into mixture. Spoon over the fruit. Bake for 35–40 minutes until golden brown and firm to the touch.

Spicy Apple Crisp

Metric/Imperial	American
filling	*filling*
675 g/1½ lbs cooking apples	1½ lbs baking apples
50 g/2 oz raisins	½ cup raisins
5 ml/1 tsp ground nutmeg	1 tsp ground netmeg
5 ml/1 tsp ground cinnamon	1 tsp ground cinnamon
pinch of ground cloves	pinch of ground cloves
150 ml/5 fl oz sweet cider	½ cup sweet cider
topping	*topping*
50 g/2 oz butter	¼ cup butter
30 ml/2 tbsps corn oil	2 tbsp corn oil
100 g/4 oz fresh, wholewheat breadcrumbs	1 cup fresh, wholewheat breadcrumbs
10 ml/2 tsps sesame seeds	2 tsps sesame seeds
15 ml/1 tbsp desiccated coconut	1 tbsp dried coconut

Preheat the oven to gas mark 4 (180°C/350°F).

Peel, core and slice the apples and place them in an ovenproof dish with alternate layers of raisins. Sprinkle with the spices and pour over the sweet cider.

To make the topping, heat the butter and oil together in a pan. Add the breadcrumbs and cook until they become golden coloured and crisp. Stir in the remaining ingredients.

Cover the apple mixture with the topping and bake for 20–25 minutes.

Summer Pudding

A classic pudding using the fresh, soft fruits of summer.

Metric/Imperial	American
450 g/1 lb mixed red fruits — blackberries, raspberries and black-currants	1 lb mixed red fruits — blackberries, raspberries and blackcurrants
275 ml/10 fl oz natural unsweetened apple and blackcurrant juice	1¼ cups natural unsweetened apple and blackcurrant juice
6–7 slices of wholewheat bread	6–7 slices of wholewheat bread

Wash and trim the fruit and simmer gently in a little of the fruit juice until tender. Drain and reserve the juice. Mix the cooking juices with the remaining fruit juice.

Cut the crusts from the bread and soak in the fruit juice for 5–8 minutes. Line a well oiled 1 litre (1¾ pint) pudding basin with most of the bread, making sure that there are no gaps in the lining.

Spoon the fruit into the basin and cover with the remaining soaked bread. Cover with a tight fitting lid or plate and stand a 1 kilo (2 lbs) weight on top. Leave for 24 hours. Turn out carefully onto a serving plate.

Thicken the remaining fruit juice with arrowroot and serve with the pudding.

Fruit Amber

A favourite family pudding — a pastry case filled with a mixture of spiced rhubarb and dates, topped with golden meringue.

Metric/Imperial	American
pastry	*pastry*
175 g/6 oz wholewheat flour	1¼ cups wholewheat flour
50 g/2 oz butter	¼ cup butter
45 ml/3 tbsps corn oil	3 tbsps corn oil
25–30 ml/5–6 tsps cold water	5–6 tsps cold water
filling	*filling*
450 g/1 lb rhubarb, chopped	1 lb rhubarb, chopped
175 g/6 oz dried dates, pitted and chopped	1½ cups dried dates, pitted and chopped
175 ml/6 fl oz water	¾ cup water
2.5 ml/½ tsp ground ginger	½ tsp ground ginger
topping	*topping*
2 egg whites	2 egg whites

Preheat the oven to gas mark 6 (200°C/400°F).

To make the pastry, place the wholewheat flour in a bowl and rub in the butter and oil until the mixture resembles breadcrumbs. Gradually add the water and press together to form a pastry dough. Roll out on a floured board and line a 17–20cm (7–8 ins) pie dish. Line the pastry with crumpled greaseproof paper and fill with dried beans. Bake for 10 minutes. Remove the dried beans and greaseproof paper and cook for a further 15 minutes. Reduce the oven temperature to gas mark ½ (120°C/250°F).

To make the filling put the rhubarb, dates and water in a pan and cook gently until the rhubarb is tender. Stir in the ground ginger and leave to cool slightly before spooning into the cooked pastry case.

Beat the egg whites until stiff and peaked, and pile on top of the fruit filling. Bake for 20–25 minutes until golden brown.

Baked Peaches

An attractive, light pudding that combines the delicate flavours of fresh peaches, oranges and almonds.

Metric/Imperial	American
4 large peaches	4 large peaches
75 g/3 oz ground almonds	¾ cup ground almonds
45 ml/3 tbsps fresh orange juice	3 tbsps fresh orange juice
150 ml/5 fl oz natural unsweetened orange juice	½ cup natural unsweetened orange juice

Preheat the oven to gas mark 5 (190°C/375°F).

Slice the top off each peach and carefully remove the stone. Mix the ground almonds with the fresh orange juice to form a stiff mixture. Stuff the peaches with the almond filling and replace the top of the fruit.

Stand the peaches in an ovenproof dish and fill with 1.25 cm (½ in) of natural unsweetened orange juice. Bake for 30 minutes until tender.

Leave to cool for 5–10 minutes before placing in individual dishes. Spoon over a little of the cooking juice before serving.

Pears Baked with Sesame Seeds

Metric/Imperial	American
4 pears	4 pears
25–50 g/1–2 oz melted butter	2–4 tbsps melted butter
25–50 g/1–2 oz sesame seeds	a scant ½ cup sesame seeds
pinch of nutmeg	pinch of nutmeg
150 ml/5 fl oz natural unsweetened apple juice	½ cup natural unsweetened apple juice

Preheat the oven to gas mark 5 (190°C/375°F).

Cut the pears in half and remove the cores. Place in an ovenproof dish and brush with melted butter. Scatter the sesame seeds on the top and sprinkle with nutmeg. Pour the apple juice into the dish to a depth of 0.75 cm (¼ in) and bake for 30–35 minutes until tender.

Baked Bananas

Metric/Imperial	American
4 firm bananas	4 firm bananas
40 g/1½ oz melted butter	3 tbsps melted butter
25–50 g/1–2 oz desiccated coconut	½ cup dried coconut

Preheat the oven to gas mark 8 (230°C/450°F).

Coat the bananas with the butter and sprinkle the desiccated coconut over the top. Place in an ovenproof dish and bake for 10–12 minutes until tender.

Crêpes with Fresh Peaches

This quantity makes ten to twelve crêpes.

Metric/Imperial	American
crêpes	*crêpes*
100 g/4 oz wholewheat flour	¾ cup wholewheat flour
pinch of salt	pinch of salt
2 medium eggs, beaten	2 medium eggs, beaten
50 g/2 oz cool melted butter	¼ cup cool melted butter
30 ml/2 tbsps soya oil	2 tbsps soy oil
30 ml/2 tbsps natural unsweetened apple juice	2 tbsps natural unsweetened apple juice
150 ml/5 fl oz milk	½ cup milk
butter or oil for frying	butter or oil for frying
filling	*filling*
100 g/4 oz natural cottage cheese	½ cup unflavoured cottage cheese
150 ml/5 fl oz sour cream	½ cup sour cream
2 ripe peaches	2 ripe peaches

To make the crêpes, mix the flour and salt together in a bowl. Make a well in the centre and add the beaten eggs. Mix the melted butter, soya oil, apple juice and milk together and gradually add to the other ingredients, stirring all the time. Beat the batter vigorously until the surface is covered with bubbles.

Heat a little butter or oil in a frying pan. When hot pour in 15 ml/1 tbsp (1 tbsp) of batter and cook on both sides until crisp and golden brown.

To make the filling, mix the cottage cheese and sour cream together. Slice the peaches.

Spoon a little of the creamy filling onto the centre of each crêpe, top with 1–2 slices of peach and serve.

Bilberry Pancakes

Bilberries are also known as blaeberries or whortleberries. They can be found on the moors, mountains and open woodlands of Europe and North America. They are juicy black–blue berries and have a delicious flavour. Bilberry pie is regarded as a real treat by my family. Bilberries are rarely sold commercially because of the tremendous effort involved in picking them. In USA the larger blueberry is more widely available and is a traditional accompaniment with pancakes and waffles.

This quantity makes ten pancakes.

Metric/Imperial	American
pancakes	*pancakes*
175 g/6 oz wholewheat flour	1¼ cups wholewheat flour
2 medium eggs, beaten	2 medium eggs, beaten
150 ml/5 fl oz milk	½ cup milk
150 ml/5 fl oz water	½ cup water
15 ml/1 tbsp soya oil	1 tbsp soy oil
pinch of salt	pinch of salt
oil for frying	oil for frying
filling	*filling*
100 g/4 oz bilberries, washed and trimmed	1 cup blueberries, washed and trimmed

Make the batter by mixing the flour and salt together in a bowl. Add the eggs. Mix the water and milk together and gradually stir into the other ingredients, beating well after each addition. Beat the batter until frothy and stir in the bilberries.

Heat a little oil in a frying pan. When hot pour in 30 ml/2 tbsps (2 tbsps) of batter. Cook quickly on both sides until golden brown.

Serve with a small bowl of fresh bilberries and natural yoghurt.

Baked Apples

Metric/Imperial	American
4 eating apples	4 eating apples
50 g/2 oz dried figs, finely chopped	½ cup dried figs, finely chopped
50 g/2 oz ground nuts	½ cup ground nuts
25 g/1 oz sunflower seeds	¼ cup sunflower seeds
25 g/1 oz butter	2 tbsps butter
150 ml/5 fl oz natural unsweetened apple juice.	½ cup natural unsweetened apple juice

Preheat the oven to gas mark 5 (190°C/375°F).

Wash and core the apples and stand them in an ovenproof dish. Mix the figs, ground nuts and sunflower seeds together and stuff into the apples. Dot a little butter over each apple. Pour the apple juice into the dish to a depth of 0.75cm (¼ in) and bake for 30–35 minutes until soft.

Desserts

Poached Plums

A classic summer dish.

Metric/Imperial	American
450 g/1 lb dessert plums	1 lb dessert plums
200 ml/7 fl oz natural unsweetened red grape juice	1 cup natural un-sweetened red grape juice
3 cloves	3 cloves
half a cinnamon stick	half a cinnamon stick

Prick the plums with a fork and place in a saucepan with the other ingredients. Bring to the boil and simmer gently for 5–10 minutes until tender. Occasionally spoon a little fruit juice over the fruit while it is cooking.

Remove the cloves and the cinnamon stick and leave to cool. Place in individual dishes and chill before serving.

A sweet red wine or port can be used in place of the grape juice.

Apricot Mousse

Metric/Imperial	American
350 g/12 oz dried apricots	3 cups dried apricots
275 ml/10 fl oz water	1¼ cups water
30 ml/2 tbsps fresh orange juice	2 tbsps fresh orange juice
150 ml/5 fl oz natural yoghurt	½ cup unflavoured yoghurt
2 egg whites	2 egg whites
to decorate	*to decorate*
1 orange	1 orange

Soak the apricots in the water overnight. Next day bring to the boil and cook gently until tender. Blend the apricots, fresh orange juice and yoghurt together until smooth and creamy. Whisk the egg whites until stiff and peaked and fold into the mixture. Spoon into individual dishes and decorate with twists of orange peel.

Continental Cheese Cake

Here is a cheese cake that can be enjoyed by everyone, even those who are watching their weight. It is delicious eaten on its own or with fresh fruit and cream. As an alternative try omitting the raisins from the recipe and baking the cheese cake in a deep flan mould. When baked and cool tip out onto a serving dish and fill the centre of the moulded cheese cake with fresh, soft fruit such as raspberries or strawberries. Serve with a cold fruit sauce.

Metric/Imperial	American
base	*base*
15 ml/1 tbsp melted butter	1 tbsp melted butter
25 g/1 oz wholewheat semolina	¼ cup wholewheat semolina flour
filling	*filling*
50 g/2 oz butter	¼ cup butter
30 ml/2 tbsps clear honey	2 tbsps clear honey
225 g/8 oz low fat cream cheese	1 cup ricotta/diet cheese
2 large eggs	2 large eggs
50 g/2 oz wholewheat semolina	½ cup wholewheat semolina flour
50 g/2 oz ground almonds	½ cup ground almonds
5 ml/1 tsp lemon zest	1 tsp grated lemon rind
75 g/3 oz raisins	½ cup raisins

Preheat the oven to gas mark 5 (190°C/375°F).

Brush a shallow, loose bottomed 17.5 cm (7 ins) cake tin with the melted butter. Line the bottom of the tin with greaseproof paper and again brush with butter. Sprinkle the 25g/1 oz (¼ cup) wholewheat semolina over the bottom of the tin.

To make the filling, cream the butter in a warm basin until smooth. Add the honey and gradually stir in the cream cheese. Separate the eggs and beat the yolks into the mixture. Add the remaining wholewheat semolina, ground almonds, lemon zest and raisins and mix together well. Beat the egg whites until stiff and fold into the mixture.

Spoon the cheese cake into the prepared tin and bake for 40–45 minutes until firm to touch. Cover the top of the cheese cake with greaseproof paper if it becomes too brown.

Leave to cool in the tin.

Peach Crème

Metric/Imperial	American
150 ml/5 fl oz single cream	½ cup light cream
275 ml/10 fl oz natural yoghurt	1¼ cups unflavoured yoghurt
15 ml/1 tbsp clear honey	1 tbsp clear honey
2.5 ml/½ tsp vanilla essence	½ tsp vanilla extract
3 egg yolks, beaten	3 egg yolks, beaten
2 large ripe peaches	2 large ripe peaches

Mix the single cream, natural yoghurt, clear honey and vanilla essence together in a small bowl. Place the bowl in a pan of warm water and heat gently until the mixture becomes lukewarm. Stir in the egg yolks and cook gently for 15 minutes, stirring frequently. Remove from the heat when the mixture is thick enough to coat the back of a spoon.

Stone and slice the peaches, reserving several slices for decoration. Lay the fruit in the bottom of individual dishes and spoon over the crème mixture. Leave in a cool place to set.

Decorate with the remaining peach slices and chill before serving.

Gooseberry Fool

Gooseberry fool is a light and refreshing summer dessert. The use of tofu instead of the more traditional ingredient, double cream, makes it popular with slimmers and those with weight problems. Try using natural yoghurt if tofu is unavailable.

Metric/Imperial	American
175 g/6 oz millet	1 cup whole hulled millet
575 ml/1 pt water	2½ cups water
225 g/8 oz ripe goose-berries	½ lb ripe gooseberries
150 ml/5 fl oz sweet cider	½ cup sweet cider
75 g/3 oz tofu	¾ cup tofu
to decorate	*to decorate*
30 ml/2 tbsps natural yoghurt	2 tbsps unflavoured yoghurt

Dry roast the millet in a pan, stirring frequently, until it becomes golden brown and smells deliciously nutty. Remove from the pan and leave to cool for 5 minutes. Return to the pan, add the water and simmer gently for 15–20 minutes until soft and fluffy. Drain if necessary.

Top and tail the gooseberries and cook gently in the cider. Blend all the ingredients together until smooth and creamy. Spoon into individual dishes and chill.

Whirl a little natural yoghurt into each dish before serving.

Peach Snow

Metric/Imperial	American
225 g/8 oz dried peaches	2 cups dried peaches
350 ml/12 fl oz natural unsweetened orange juice juice and grated rind of 2 oranges	1½ cups natural un-sweetened orange juice juice and grated rind of 2 oranges
3 egg whites	3 egg whites

Soak the peaches in the orange juice overnight. Next day cook the fruit in the juice until soft. Add the juice of the 2 oranges and blend until smooth. Leave to cool.

Beat the egg whites until stiff and fold into the fruit purée. Spoon into individual dishes and sprinkle with the grated orange rind.

Serve chilled.

Banana and Carob Mousse

A light, low calorie mousse.

Metric/Imperial	American
2 medium ripe bananas	2 medium ripe bananas
20 ml/4 tsps carob flour	4 tsps carob flour
50 g/2 oz low fat cream cheese	¼ cup ricotta/diet cheese
45 ml/3 tbsps natural yoghurt	3 tbsps unflavoured yoghurt
3 medium eggs, separated	3 medium eggs, separated
1 egg yolk	1 egg yolk

Blend the bananas, carob flour, cream cheese, natural yoghurt and the egg yolks together. Place the mixture in a small bowl, over a pan of water and heat gently for 15 minutes, stirring frequently until the mixture begins to thicken. When it is sufficiently thick to coat the back of a spoon remove from the heat.

Beat the egg whites until stiff and fold into the creamed mixture. Place in individual dishes.

Serve chilled.

Blackberry Foam

An attractive fresh dessert that is light and refreshing.

Metric/Imperial	American
450 g/1 lb ripe blackberries	1 lb ripe blackberries
2 egg whites	2 egg whites

Rub the blackberries through a sieve to remove the seeds. Beat the egg whites until stiff and fold into the fruit purée.

Serve immediately.

Dried Fruit Compote

Metric/Imperial	American
50 g/2 oz dried pears	½ cup dried pears
50 g/2 oz dried prunes	½ cup dried prunes
50 g/2 oz dried apricots	½ cup dried apricots
50 g/2 oz dried peaches	½ cup dried peaches
50 g/2 oz dried apple	½ cup dried apple
3 cloves	3 cloves
1 stick of cinnamon	1 stick cinnamon
the zest of 1 large orange	grated rind of 1 large orange

Cover the fruit with water and bring to the boil. Remove from the heat, cover and leave to stand for 1 hour. Drain and reserve the juice. Add 425 ml/15 fl oz (1¾ cups) of the reserved juice, the cloves and cinnamon stick to the fruit and bring to the boil. Simmer gently for 30 minutes until the fruit is soft.

Chill and sprinkle with orange zest before serving.

Pashka Cheese Cake

A light and creamy moulded dessert eaten during Easter celebrations in parts of Eastern Europe. An authentic pashka mould is pyramid shaped and stamped with holy symbols and Easter greetings. A coeur de crème dish, sieve or new flower pot can be used in its place. Pashka is similar in taste and texture to a cheese cake but is cheaper and easier to prepare and contains fewer calories.

This quantity serves four to five.

Metric/Imperial	American
350 g/12 oz natural cottage cheese	1½ cups unflavoured cottage cheese
15 ml/1 tbsp natural yoghurt	1 tbsp unflavoured yoghurt
25 g/1 oz mixed peel	1 tbsp mixed peel
25 g/1 oz currants	1 tbsp currants
25 g/1 oz raisins	1 tbsp raisins
25 g/1 oz walnuts, chopped	1 tbsp walnuts, chopped
25 g/1 oz butter, melted	2 tbsps butter, melted
½ egg, beaten	½ egg, beaten
juice and grated rind of 1 orange	juice and grated rind of 1 orange
a few drops of vanilla essence	a few drops of vanilla extract
a pinch of mixed spice	a pinch of mixed spice

Drain the cottage cheese and rub it through a sieve into a bowl. Add all the other ingredients and mix together well. Line a suitable mould with butter muslin, leaving sufficient material to fold over the top. Fill the mould with the mixture, cover with the muslin and place a 1 kg (2 lbs) weight on the top. Stand on a plate in a cool place for twelve hours.

Turn out of the mould, remove the cloth and place on a serving dish. Decorate with toasted nuts or fresh fruit.

Minted Fruit Salad

Metric/Imperial	American
2 oranges	2 oranges
3 kiwi fruit	3 kiwi fruit
225 g/8 oz seedless green grapes	½ lb seedless white grapes
15–30 ml/1–2 tbsps fresh mint, chopped	1–2 tbsps fresh mint, chopped
150 ml/5 fl oz natural unsweetened apple juice	½ cup natural unsweetened apple juice

Peel and slice the oranges and kiwi fruit. Wash the grapes and remove the stalks. Mix the fruit together with the mint and place in a serving bowl. Pour over the fruit juice and chill before serving.

Three Fruit Medley

Metric/Imperial	American
1 small honeydew melon	1 small honeydew melon
225 g/8 oz raspberries	½ lb raspberries
2 kiwi fruit	2 kiwi fruit
the juice of 2 lemons	the juice of 2 lemons

Cut the melon into cubes, wash the raspberries and peel and slice the kiwi fruit. Mix all the fruits together and place in a serving bowl. Pour over the lemon juice and chill before serving.

The scooped–out shell of the melon makes an attractive and unusual serving dish.

Apple Snow

Metric/Imperial	American
4 medium Cox's eating apples	4 medium Cox's eating apples
5–10 ml/1–2 tsps lemon zest	1–2 tsps grated lemon rind
2 egg whites	2 egg whites

Slice the apples and cook them with a little water until soft. Rub the apples through a sieve or a food mill to form a smooth purée. Stir in the lemon zest. Leave to cool. Beat the egg whites until stiff and fold into the apple purée. Pile into individual glasses.

Serve immediately.

Watermelon Basket

Mark Twain is said to have described the watermelon as 'the food that angels eat'. Certainly the sweet red flesh of the watermelon when mixed with fresh strawberries and raspberries in this dessert looks tempting enough.

Metric/Imperial	American
1 small watermelon	1 small watermelon
1 punnet of strawberries	1 punnet of strawberries
225 g/8 oz raspberries	1½ cups raspberries

Cut the watermelon in half and scoop the seeds from one of the segments. Remove the flesh with a melon baller and place in a mixing bowl, retaining as much juice as possible. Pull the stalks from the strawberries and raspberries. Mix together with the watermelon balls. Spoon the fruit into the hollowed watermelon. Pour over any remaining juice. Chill before serving.

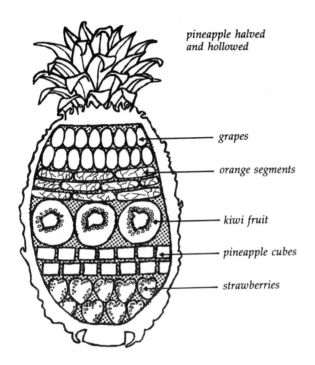

pineapple halved
and hollowed

grapes

orange segments

kiwi fruit

pineapple cubes

strawberries

Pineapple Boat

Kiwi fruit are also known as chinese gooseberries. The brown furry skin covers bright green flesh that is patterned with decorative edible seeds.

Metric/Imperial	American
1 pineapple	1 pineapple
75 g/3 oz green grapes	½ cup white grapes
1 large orange	1 large orange
2 kiwi fruit	2 kiwi fruit
75 g/3 oz strawberries	½ cup strawberries

Cut the pineapple in half from top to bottom, leaving the leaves attached. Scoop out the flesh and cut into cubes. Wash the grapes and remove the stalks. Peel the orange and cut the membrane from each segment. Peel and slice the kiwi fruit. Pull the stalks from the strawberries. Cut a thin slice from the bottom of one of the pineapple halves so that the boat can stand steady.

Fill three quarters of the boat with pineapple cubes. Starting from the leafy top arrange a row of grapes across the partially filled pineapple. Then add a row of orange segments. Follow this with a row of kiwi fruit, a row of pineapple cubes and finally a row of strawberries. Place the pineapple on a flat serving dish and pile the remaining fruit around its base.

Serve with a cream dip.

Mango Fool

The bright pinky-golden flesh of ripe mangoes is smooth and creamy and has a delicate flavour. Buy mangoes when they are just soft — those that are completely green tend to be underripe while those mottled with large black marks are generally past their best.

Metric/Imperial	American
2 large ripe mangoes	2 large ripe mangoes
15 ml/1 tbsp lemon juice	1 tbsp lemon juice
150 ml/5 fl oz natural yoghurt	½ cup unflavoured yoghurt
150 ml/5 fl oz double cream	½ cup heavy cream

Peel and stone the mangoes. Put all the ingredients in a blender and liquidise until smooth. Pour into 4 small individual glasses and chill before serving.

Melon with Grapes and Lychees

Metric/Imperial	American
1 cantaloupe melon	1 cantaloupe melon
100 g/4 oz black grapes	¾ cup black grapes
10 fresh lychees	10 fresh lychees
juice of 1 large lime	juice of 1 large lime

Cut the melon in half and remove the flesh with a melon baller. Place the melon balls and black grapes in a serving bowl. Peel the lychees and add to the fruit bowl. Pour over the lime juice and chill before serving.

Strawberry Yoghurt

Metric/Imperial	American
125 ml/4 fl oz natural unsweetened apple juice	½ cup natural unsweetened apple juice
75 g/3 oz sultanas	½ cup white seedless raisins
450 g/1 lb strawberries	1 lb strawberries
350 ml/12 fl oz natural yoghurt	1½ cups unflavoured yoghurt

Put the apple juice and sultanas in a small pan and bring to the boil. Simmer gently for 10 minutes. Leave to cool. Place in a blender with half the strawberries and the yoghurt. Liquidise until smooth. Stir in the remaining ingredients and chill before serving.

Apple and Hazelnut Yoghurt

Metric/Imperial	American
125 ml/4 fl oz natural unsweetened apple juice	½ cup natural unsweetened apple juice
450 g/1 lb apples, cored and sliced	1 lb apples, cored and sliced
425 ml/15 fl oz natural yoghurt	1¾ cups unflavoured yoghurt
5 ml/1 tsp lemon zest	1 tsp grated lemon rind
50 g/2 oz roasted hazelnuts	½ cup roasted hazelnuts

Place the apple juice and apple slices in a pan. Bring to the boil and cook for 5–10 minutes. Put the apples in a blender and add the yoghurt. Stir in the lemon zest. Chop the hazelnuts and mix into the apple yoghurt. Chill before serving.

Peaches and Raspberries in Orange Juice

Metric/Imperial	American
450 g/1 lb raspberries	3 cups raspberries
2 large peaches	2 large peaches
150 ml/5 fl oz fresh orange juice	½ cup fresh orange juice

Remove the stalks from the raspberries and place in a serving dish. Slice the peaches, discard the stones and mix with the raspberries. Pour over the orange juice and chill before serving.

Fresh Figs with Orange

All the fig is edible and they make a delicious dessert. The orange juice used in this recipe complements their delicate flavour perfectly but do not chill before serving.

Metric/Imperial	American
4 fresh, ripe figs	4 fresh, ripe figs
the zest and juice of 2 oranges	the grated rind and juice of 2 oranges

Cut each fig into four segments and place on individual serving dishes. Mix the orange zest and juice together and spoon over the figs. Serve.

Rum and Raisin Ice

Metric/Imperial	American
225 g/8 oz raisins	1½ cups raisins
150 ml/5 fl oz double cream	½ cup heavy cream
150 ml/5 fl oz natural yoghurt	½ cup unflavoured yoghurt
45 ml/3 tbsps carob flour	3 tbsps carob flour
5–10 ml/1–2 tsps rum	1–2 tsps rum
3 large egg whites	3 large egg whites

Pound the raisins until they become a smooth paste. Stir in the cream, yoghurt, carob flour and rum. Beat the egg whites until stiff and peaked. Fold into the mixture. Place in 4 individual freezerproof dishes and freeze until firm. Put in the refrigerator for 30 minutes before serving.

Raspberry Yoghurt Ice

A delicious ice cream that is very easy to prepare.

Metric/Imperial	American
225 g/8 oz raspberries	½ lb raspberries
575 ml/1 pt natural yoghurt	2½ cups unflavoured yoghurt

Rub the raspberries through a sieve to remove the seeds. Mix the fruit and yoghurt together and place in a freezer-proof container. Freeze. Stir the ice cream thoroughly every hour until it has the consistency of crushed ice.

Prune Whip

Metric/Imperial
350 g/12 oz prunes
275 ml/10 fl oz cold tea
30 ml/2 tbsps fresh
orange juice
100 g/4 oz tofu
2 large egg whites

to decorate
15 g/1 tbsp flaked
almonds

American
3 cups prunes
1¼ cups cold tea
2 tbsps fresh orange juice
1 cup tofu
2 large egg whites

to decorate
1 tbsp flaked almonds

Soak the prunes overnight in the cold tea.
Next day cook the fruit in the tea until soft.
Drain and reserve the juice. Stone the prunes
and blend with the orange juice, tofu and 90
ml/6 tbsps (6 tbsps) of prune juice.

Beat the egg whites until stiff and fold into
the creamy mixture. Spoon into the individual
dishes and sprinkle with the flaked almonds.

Chill before serving.

Fresh Fruit Mould

Metric/Imperial
450 g/1 lb fresh fruit
(raspberries, bananas,
peaches, grapes etc)
10 ml/2 tsps agar agar
575 ml/1 pt natural
unsweetened red grape
juice

American
1 lb fresh fruit
(raspberries, bananas,
peaches, grapes etc)
2 tsps agar agar
2½ cups natural
unsweetened red grape
juice

Wash, trim and chop the fruit and place in a
mould. Blend the agar agar with 60 ml/4 tbsps
(4 tbsps) of cold fruit juice. Add the remaining
fruit juice and pour into a pan. Bring to the boil.
Simmer gently for 1–2 minutes, stirring
frequently. Leave to cool slightly before
pouring over the fruit. Unlike gelatine agar agar
sets when tepid. Pour over the fruit as soon as
it begins to thicken.

Chill until set.

Petit Fours and Snacks

Here are a number of recipes which provide an attractive and delicious alternative to traditional, sugar laden petit fours. They can be served after a meal or in place of sweets and chocolates. The savoury snacks may be served with predinner drinks.

Sesame Delights

Metric/Imperial	American
100 g/4 oz dried dates, pitted and chopped	1 cup dried dates, pitted and chopped
50 g/2 oz raisins	½ cup raisins
25 g/1 oz walnuts, chopped	¼ cup walnuts, chopped
20 ml/4 tsps carob flour	4 tsps carob flour
25 g/1 oz sesame seeds, lightly roasted	¼ cup sesame seeds, lightly roasted

Pound the dates and raisins together to form a stiff paste. Add the walnuts and carob flour and work the mixture together with the fingertips. Roll into small balls and coat in the sesame seeds.

To roast the sesame seeds, place them in a pan over a high heat. Cook them, stirring constantly until they begin to 'pop' and turn a slightly darker colour.

Stuffed Prunes

Metric/Imperial	American
225 g/8 oz prunes	2 cups prunes
90 ml/6 tbsps ground almonds	6 tbsps ground almonds
30 ml/2 tbsps fresh orange juice	2 tbsps fresh orange juice

Soak the prunes overnight in water. Next day cook the prunes in the water until soft. Drain and remove the prune stones carefully. Dry the fruit with a clean kitchen towel. Mix the ground almonds and orange juice together to form a paste. Fill the prunes with the almond mixture and place in paper sweet cases.

Fresh, stoned dates can be used instead of the prunes.

Dream Balls

Metric/Imperial	American
225 g/8 oz dried dates, pitted and chopped	2 cups dried dates, pitted and chopped
1 ripe banana, mashed	1 ripe banana, mashed
50 g/2 oz hazelnuts, chopped	½ cup hazelnuts, chopped
100 g/4 oz desiccated coconut	2 cups dried coconut

Pound the dates to a stiff paste. Add the mashed banana and chopped hazelnuts and mix together well. Form into small balls and coat with desiccated coconut. Place in paper sweet cases.

Apricot Creams

Metric/Imperial	American
100 g/4 oz low fat cream cheese	½ cup ricotta/diet cheese
1.25 ml/¼ tsp ground ginger	¼ tsp ground ginger
5–10 ml/1–2 tsps orange zest	1–2 tsps granted orange rind
225 g/8 oz whole, dried dessert apricots	2 cups whole, dried dessert apricots

Mix the cream cheese, ground ginger and orange zest together in a bowl. Carefully cut open the apricots and remove the stones. Stuff with the creamy filling. Place in paper sweet cases.

Fresh dessert apricots can be used when in season.

Roasted Peanuts and Sunflower Seeds

A crunchy, savoury snack to eat after a meal or in place of sweets and chocolates.

Metric/Imperial	American
100 g/4 oz peanuts	1 cup peanuts
100 g/4 oz sunflower seeds	1 cup sunflower seeds
30 ml/2 tbsps shoyu soya sauce	2 tbsps shoyu soy sauce

Preheat the oven to gas mark 5 (190°C/375°F).

Mix all the ingredients together in a bowl. Leave aside for 30 minutes. Spread the peanuts and sunflower seeds on a lightly oiled baking tray and cook for 30 minutes. Turn occasionally during cooking to ensure even roasting.

Salted Almonds

A traditional accompaniment to predinner drinks.

Metric/Imperial	American
225 g/8 oz almonds	2 cups almonds
white of 1 egg	white of 1 egg
salt	salt

Many recipes suggest frying the almonds in a little oil but I find this leaves them too oily. It is much better to roast them slowly in a moderate oven (gas mark 4 180°C/350°F) until they become a pale golden colour. The outer skins can then be removed quite easily while the almonds are still warm by rubbing them in a clean towel.

When the almonds are cool coat them in egg white and fine salt. They are best eaten soon after preparation but will keep for a short time in an airtight container.

Sauces

Plum Sauce

Metric/Imperial
4 large dessert plums
225 g/8 oz low fat cream cheese
30–45 ml/2–3 tbsps natural yoghurt

American
4 large dessert plums
1 cup ricotta/diet cheese
2–3 tbsps unflavoured yoghurt

Stone the plums and blend all the ingredients together until smooth and creamy. Chill before serving.

Banana Cream

Metric/Imperial
4 ripe bananas
275 ml/10 fl oz natural yoghurt

American
4 ripe bananas
1¼ cups unflavoured yoghurt

Blend the ingredients together until smooth and creamy. Chill before serving.

Mock Chocolate Sauce

Metric/Imperial
225 g/8 oz prunes
275 ml/10 fl oz water
5 ml/1 tsp carob flour
225 g/8 oz natural cottage cheese
10 ml/2 tsps natural yoghurt

American
2 cups prunes
1¼ cups water
1 tsp carob flour
1 cup unflavoured cottage cheese
2 tsps unflavoured yoghurt

Soak the prunes overnight in water. Next day cook them gently until tender. Drain and leave to cool. Remove the stones and blend the prunes with the carob flour and cottage cheese. Add sufficient natural yoghurt to give a smooth creamy consistency.

Try using tofu instead of the cottage cheese and yoghurt.

Fresh Fruit Cream

A delicious cream to serve with fruit desserts.

Metric/Imperial	American
75 g/3 oz wholewheat semolina	¾ cup wholewheat semolina flour
1 large ripe banana, peeled	1 large banana, peeled
1 large eating apple, cored and sliced	1 large eating apple, cored and sliced
250 ml/9 fl oz water	1 cup water
2.5 ml/½ tsp vanilla essence	½ tsp vanilla extract

Blend all the ingredients together until smooth and creamy.

Prune Cream

Metric/Imperial	American
100 g/4 oz prunes	1 cup prunes
150 ml/5 fl oz water	½ cup water
30 ml/2 tbsps ground nuts	2 tbsps ground nuts
125 ml/5 fl oz natural yoghurt	½ cup unflavoured yoghurt

Soak the prunes overnight in water. Next day cook gently until soft. Drain and reserve the juice. Remove the stones and blend the fruit, ground nuts and natural yoghurt together. Add sufficient prune juice to give a smooth creamy consistency.

Cashewnut Cream

This makes an excellent 'dip' to serve with a dish of assorted fresh fruit slices. It makes an attractive finish to an evening meal.

Metric/Imperial	American
100 g/4 oz cashewnuts	1 cup cashewnuts
125–150 ml/4–5 fl oz water	a scant ½ cup water

Grind the cashewnuts and blend them with the water. Rub through a sieve for a really smooth cream.

Hot Orange Sauce

Metric/Imperial	American
25 g/1 oz butter	2 tbsps butter
30 ml/2 tbsps unbleached white flour	2 tbsps unbleached white flour
225 ml/8 fl oz natural unsweetened orange juice	1 cup natural unsweetened orange juice
1 large orange, peeled and chopped	1 large orange, peeled and chopped

Melt the butter in a pan. Stir in the flour and cook gently for a minute or two over a low flame. Remove from the heat and gradually add the orange juice, stirring well after each addition. Return to the heat and cook gently, stirring all the time until the sauce is thick and smooth. Add the chopped fruit and serve.

Hot Fruit Sauce

Metric/Imperial
3 peaches
6 dessert plums
150 ml/5 fl oz natural
unsweetened apple juice

American
3 peaches
6 dessert plums
½ cup natural un-
sweetened apple juice

Stone and chop the fruit and place in a pan with the apple juice. Simmer for 10 minutes until tender. Blend the ingredients together until smooth. Thicken with a little arrowroot if desired. Serve.

Index

General Index

Agar agar 24,65
Apricots 17
Arrowroot 24,66

Baking:
  biscuits 22-23
  cakes 21
  pastry 22
  scones 23
Batter:
  crêpes 75
  pancakes 31, 75
Biscuits 22-23, 41, 42, 43
Blind baking 24
Blood sugar 9, 10, 11, 19
Buttermilk 37

Caffeine 15
Cakes 21, 44-59
Calcium 14, 15, 18
Carbohydrates 9, 10
Carob 5, 15, 24
Chromium 15, 16
Concentrated fruit juice 24
Copper 15
Curd 24, 61
Currants 17
Cyclamates 19

Dates 5, 17
Degenerative diseases 8, 10, 19
Demerara sugar 14
Diabetes 8, 11
Disaccharides 10
Dried fruit 17, 18, 19, 24
Dry roasting 24, 87

Energy 9

Fat 9
Fibre 8, 13, 17, 19, 25
Figs 18, 85
Fresh fruit 19
Fructose 10, 11, 15, 16

Galactose 10
Glucose 10, 11, 15, 16

Honey 5, 7, 15, 19

Insulin 11
Iron 15, 16, 17, 18

Kiwi fruit 24, 83

Lactose 10,
Laxatives 16, 17, 18
Low fat cream cheese 24

Maize meal 24
Malt extract 15, 19
Maltose 10
Mango 84
Marzipan 53
Meringue 73
Migraine 15
Millet 25
Minerals 9, 13, 14, 15, 16, 17, 18
Miso 25
Molasses 15, 19
Molasses sugar 14
Monosaccharides 10
Muscovado sugar 14

Natural unsweetened fruit juice 25
Nutrients 9, 13, 14, 15, 16, 17, 18

Obesity 5, 8, 11, 19
Oils 25

Pancreas 11